YOU'VE GOT THE

POWER

A Six-Week Hero's Journey to
Increased Confidence and Happiness

PAULA PLUCK

lotus
publishing

Chichester, England

First published in 2020 by

Lotus Publishing

Apple Tree Cottage, Inlands Road, Nutbourne, Chichester, PO18 8RJ

Text Design Medlar Publishing Solutions Pvt Ltd., India

Cover Design Alissa Dinallo

Illustrations Samuel Cox

Printed and Bound in India by Replika Press

Disclaimer

This book is not intended as a substitute for the medical advice of a physician. The carer/reader should regularly consult a physician in matters relating to mental health issues and particularly with respect to any symptoms that may require diagnosis or medical attention.

Although both the author and the publisher have made every effort to ensure that the information in this book was correct at the time of going to print, the author and publisher do not assume and hereby disclaim any liability to any party for any loss, damage, or disruption caused by errors or omissions, whether such errors or omissions result from negligence, accident, or any other cause.

British Library Cataloging-in-Publication Data

A CIP record for this book is available from the British Library

ISBN 978 1 913088 04 0

ACKNOWLEDGEMENTS

For all the teachers and schools I've worked with delivering the SMART Young Minds mindfulness and resilience training in schools and community settings project. For the awesome teachers, who are SMART-trained coaches: you are all literally responsible for making this book happen.

Thanks to my dear friend Kush Kumar for introducing my work to Lotus Publishing. To my lovely publishers at Lotus – Jon, thanks so much for believing in the vision for this book, and Hannah, thanks for being a fabulous guide all the way through – you've got the power! Thanks to the lovely, patient Maia Vaswani, my editor. Thanks to Samuel for his amazing illustrations that bring this coaching book to life.

CONTENTS

Contents

DEDICATION

For Ben and Dan

You are the heart of my world

Love you

Mum

INTRODUCTION

Hey there!

I'm Paula and I am going to be mentoring you through the next six weeks. It's fantastic that you are here, we are going to have an awesome time.

You're holding dynamite – this book could literally blow up your world in a great way; nothing dangerous, mind, just a brilliant new way of seeing and living. What's involved, I hear you cry? Well, I'm going to teach you about your tremendous inner powers so you can unleash your brilliance on the world. Getting good at stuff and feeling happier and more confident are easier than you might think. 'You've got the Power' is the GPS on your hero's journey for getting better at almost anything.

Who wouldn't want to know how to tap into the superpowers of self-confidence, happiness, freedom and being great at just about anything? If you like the idea of that, then this book is for you. If you have a mate who seems amazing at everything or if your brother or sister is the bright one, the sporty one, the arty one, the talented one, then this book is for you. If you haven't found your groove yet and you're not sure what you're best at – you've got it, this book is for you.

It only takes six weeks, so we haven't got time to waste – the sooner we get started, the sooner you can step into your power and stand out from the crowd, proud of your identity. Your endgame may be to be an astronaut, superstar singer, entrepreneur tycoon, teacher, surgeon, football player or just about anything, and this book will help you get the mindset to get closer to that vision. More importantly, it will take you day by day through how to overcome the challenges you'll meet on the way, in the everyday stuff you are faced with in life.

You might be feeling low in the confidence department and want to plug into a little power, or hurt because the school bully has you in their sights. Maybe you just want to improve your game at maths or learn how to do a headstand in the short term. Whatever it is, we'll bust the myths that keep you stuck in a worry mindset and dive deep into the power that will have you bursting with courage, confidence, compassion, connection, creativity and a caring attitude that rocks POWER.

It's exciting, isn't it? What's involved? It's pretty straightforward, actually: you turn up daily, do the practice and feel great. What's not to like? We'll occasionally stretch your comfort zone on your six-week hero's journey, delving into what makes the brain tick; personal responsibility; owning your amazing, unique, talented self; the butterfly effect; an attitude of gratitude; and, of course, blowing up those old limitations with your dynamite new way of thinking!

Up for it? Great. Let's get this show on the road to a more successful and happy life.

P.S. You'll need a journal for the next 42 days to chart your journey. *Cool fact: Douglas Adams, the author of the Hitchhiker's Guide to the Galaxy, coined 42 as the almighty answer to the meaning of life, the universe and everything. Pretty cool, we could be onto something here ...*

WEEK ONE

THE POWER MINDSET

ACT ONE – SEPARATION

- ✔ The hero's journey
- ✔ The call to adventure
- ✔ From worry to wonder

---

*The choice to be excellent begins with
aligning your thoughts and your words with
the intention to require more from yourself.*

—Oprah Winfrey

The hero's journey

You're next

WELCOME TO YOUR NEW POWERFUL LIFE!

Week one: Your call to adventure ...

Are you ready for a new adventure?

If you must fidget, do it now! Your mission, if you choose to accept it, is to play the starring role in this hero's journey. If you are up for the challenge, you'll need to be switched on and pay careful attention to everything you see, think, feel and hear, no matter how unusual it may seem. Please be warned: if you want to stand out from the crowd and feel more confident and brilliant, if you look away even for an instant then you, our hero, will surely forget, **you've got the power!**

Today is the first day for you to get to know your power mindset and ditch those can't-do worries. We'll be moving from worry to wonder, and you will start working your power right off the bat. What's involved, I hear you ask? Well, this week is all about awareness. We'll be getting up close and personal with what makes you tick, checking out the key players in the brain, and asking is it worry or wonder that leads the show in your life.

Imagine if you could create a mindset (way of thinking) that could help you achieve your dreams. Now that's **power**. I am not talking about instant celebrity overnight, becoming the next Steve Jobs or creating a cure for cancer – all good dreams, by the way. I am talking more about having the confidence to go on stage at school, try out for that sporting position, make new friends, enter a writing competition or raise your game in maths.

We can train our brains to achieve our ambition and make our dreams come true. Our brains are awesome and when we get that, training them and good old-fashioned practice make it easy, even when it's hard! It all comes down to inspiring yourself and believing you can feel the confidence you need to achieve what you want. Yes, even those dreams that make you smile and feel warm inside – we all have them.

Great choice ... *For whatever reason, you've decided you're going to give this adventure a go. It could be a skateboard or sparkly shoes, I don't know (reveal coming in Act One). What I do know is it's fair to say, right at this point,* **'You've Got the Power'***, and that's pretty awesome.*

You're not alone on this adventure! There are calls to adventure going on all over the cosmos. A couple I quite like closer to home are Harry's and Olivia's – we'll check in on them soon.

THE HERO'S JOURNEY

Life is an unstoppable, awesome journey of highs and lows. Great minds all over the planet have pondered its meaning since the beginning of time. I love how Joseph Campbell describes it: he coined life as the '**Hero's Journey**'. We can live our life in many ways. The hero's journey is about a quest to go beyond the limits of the present world and create a greater sense of happiness in life by connecting to the all-powerful universe in and around you and me.

Are you ready? It's time to break free from your usual life. You will be moving from the ordinary to the extraordinary, from the known to the unknown world, from worry to wonder. This is your **new beginning**. Many have gone before you on the hero's quest and many will come after you. Even the great film-maker George Lucas used the hero's journey as the basis for the amazing Star Wars movies! You see, whether you call it 'the power' or 'the force', **you've got it!**

This may be news to you, but the hero's journey is acted out in everyday life in some form by all of us. Whether you're raising money for a heart-stirring, hard-hitting cause, or you're called to be a hero daily as a carer. Whether you suffer from a personal illness or you have a vision to gain a national time at your favourite sporting event, there will always be cycles of the journey at play. The journey has three main acts: **separation**, **initiation** and the **return**. Each act calls you to delve into the deeper nature of yourself, taking you through the mysterious, magical manifestation of powers in you:

1. In the first act you will face the **separation** phase; here you will first hear your call to adventure, fearlessly going from the known to the unknown world of *you*. It's time to say yes to your big adventure, your new beginning. As you experience the death of the old you may have the odd wobble accepting **you've got the power** to cross the threshold into your new world of adventure. It's normal to be tempted to refuse the call, but I will be with you, inspiring you to give it a go.

2. The second act will get a bit juicy as you come face to face with your fears, and before your **initiation** there will be ordeals and rewards – and you will survive. You'll face the dragons of worry thinking and slay them with your wonder power. You are learning to follow your heart, your bliss. Like any hero you will meet your mentor(s) and encounter supernatural aid. You will begin to see that you can choose love over fear or courage over worry or kindness over anxiety. This is because **you've got the power** and you're beginning to believe it!

3. Act three will see the death of the old ways that held you back from your incredible self. You will ascend from the worry world and awaken into your new way of thinking and feeling with increased happiness and confidence. You will be called to sacrifice some unhealthy habits and **return** a hero, transformed as the master of your mind and the director of your future. You've got this!

We must be willing to let go of
the life we planned so as to have
the life that is waiting for us.

—Joseph Campbell

Our hero's journey is all about a radical new way of thinking, acting and understanding the world. As the hero in our story, you will be called to boldly go on a breathtaking journey. It doesn't get any better than this. Sure, it will be filled with many challenges and surprises, but eventually you will end up making a brilliant contribution to life as you unleash your incredible new powers into the world. Let's do this!

ACT ONE – THE BRAVE NEW WORLD

Ordinary world: Alright, this is all about your normal life at the start of the story, before the adventure begins. The hero's journey always begins and ends in our normal life. Problems and challenges in life call us to have the courage to take a risk, make a change or just become a bit more awesome. You start questioning your potential and whether you're living up to it – maybe you're stuck in routines and don't necessarily challenge the status quo. You follow the rules, which is not all bad, but deep down you just think there must be more to life.

Call to adventure: OK, this is about your destiny. The universe is summoning you to rise to the challenge of greatness. As we go about our lives, we'll get the call to embark on quests a lot. The thing is, most of us ignore the call, we play it safe and miss out on our dreams, our call to greatness. We might back out of the school play or not try out for a quiz or sport for fear of being rejected. This can lead to feelings of boredom and anxiety, trying to figure out what it's all about – you get frustrated, resulting in '**I-am-not-enough thoughts**'.

There you have it. You the hero are living your life in the familiar usual way, when suddenly you receive a mysterious invitation, a call to adventure. Typically, you'll have to face your fears or stretch your comfort zone to pick up the challenge, and this means change and letting go of the familiar. *You've Got the Power* is asking you to leave the common world of worry and enter into the special world of wonder and greatness.

Refusal of the call: Listen, change is scary, right? Maybe you feel a bit low in the confidence department? You may be tempted to refuse this call, worrying it's too hard. As humans, we like the familiar, so expect a few attempts to refuse the adventure because of fear, worry, insecurity or resistance. It's totally understandable, so don't worry – it happens to us all. I'll be showing you how to face your fears or step up to those challenges that feel too risky. Gone are the days where you miss out on a great opportunity and wonder what could have been!

Meeting with the mentor: **You've Got the Power** is full of wisdom, insights and guidance, along with loads of feel-great practices that will fuel you with power and courage, every step of the way on your journey. Think of your life as a new blockbuster movie starring you. Why not? In *The Hobbit* Frodo had Gandalf; in *Star Wars* Luke Skywalker meets Obi-Wan Kenobi; Katniss had Haymitch in *The Hunger Games* and Dorothy in *The Wizard of Oz* meets Glinda, the Good Witch of the South. A friend, relative or teacher may take on the mentor role too and become a trusted advisor you can get support from along the way, as well as from me in this book. Time to meet a couple of other warriors of change starting their own journey too.

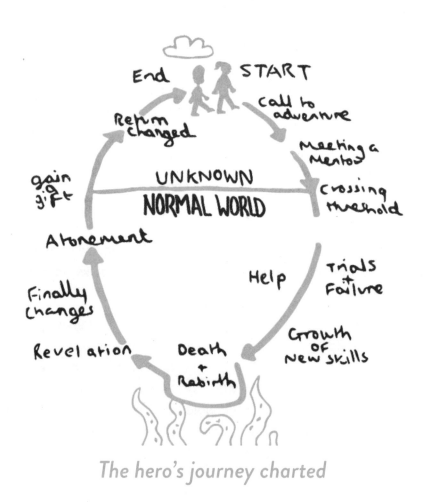

The hero's journey charted

THIS IS ACT ONE FOR HARRY FROM LIVERPOOL

Harry's mum beams, 'You're gonna love this bouk,' wildly pushing a book in his face.

Harry notices she looks slightly deranged ... He then spots the word 'power', thinking, 'Gawd, here we go ... Stop trying to fix me, I'm not a loner, I'd just rather me Xbox over a belt from Snake if it's all the same to you. THANKS.'

'It's brilliant, Harry, and you'll get to star in it,' she gushed. 'It's like a hero's journey, you know, you could be like that lad Luke Skywalker, from thingamajig, what is it? Yeah, that's right, *Star Wars*, and you love him, don't you, Harry?'

'Oh gawd,' Harry thought again, saying, 'Mum, I hate this self, whatsit, improvement stuff and I'd rather eat kale, ta very much.' He lied ...

'Arrh, don't be like that, love, maybe, just maybe, you'll love it!'

'But, mum, it'll be sooo boring! I'll hate it.' He believed it!

'It'll only take 42 days to finish; if you do it I'll getcha a skateboard,' she pleaded.

'OMG, 42 days is forever,' he said, at the same time thinking, 'I do want a skateboard ...' (the hook). In honesty, he didn't think anything could stop Snake, especially a bouk! Ruby, his mum, was waiting, holding her breath. 'I'd better say yes before she faints,' he thought! 'Erh, okay then.' 'God, I must really want that skateboard,' he thought.

'That's great, babe, I'm made up for you, are you made up?'

He really wanted this to stop, so he mumbled, 'Yeah,' or she'd never get out of his room. She was now hugging him like he was a hero going off to war. 'Mum, get off, will yeh? I've said I'll read it!'

Not for the first time, he wondered would she worry so much if she and his dad hadn't got divorced. Pushing that from his mind he thought, 'Stop, Harry. One challenge at a time.'

Albeit reluctantly, Harry, our hero, accepts his call to adventure!

Paula thinks:

Harry has the stress of being bullied playing on his mind a lot here. It looks like he is staying in more to avoid any close encounters with Snake. Practising mindful meditation and breath awareness in the next few days will really help calm his stress.

We also learn his parents have divorced, which will have an impact on how he is feeling and thinking. As Harry begins to understand how the brain works in the next week he'll be able to start self-regulating his thoughts and feelings to reduce stress.

You've Got the Power will challenge Harry to stand up to his bully through various strategies such as enlisting help, reasoning or making a stand, which will empower Harry to feel more confident and resilient in himself. It will also help him come to terms with his parents' divorce and resolve any sadness or grief he is still holding on to.

As Harry begins to integrate his superpower strategies and think like a hero, he will create a powerful mindset where he knows he makes a difference and he will start valuing himself and create healthy boundaries. As Harry starts changing his words, his mindset will change from worry to wonder and his reality will start getting better, because changing our words changes our world.

We'll be keeping an eye on Harry over the next six weeks, checking in with how he's getting on. No spoilers follow, but I'm pretty sure everyone in the world knows this adventure's big reveal is …

THIS IS ACT ONE FOR OLIVIA FROM BRIGHTON (WELL, HOVE ACTUALLY)

Olivia is 12 and doesn't fancy anyone, even though all her mates do. She's stuck between the glamour of the latest fashions and channelling the next universal genius.

Today, her usually lovely Pops is really annoying her, rattling on about something or another, including growing pains! To his and her surprise, she yells, 'It's not growing pains, Pops, it's something else. It makes me ... oh ... I don't know. I don't want it – I hate it!'

'What, darling?' said Pops, feeling way out of his depth.

'I don't know ...', said Olivia with tears spilling down her face. And the truth was she didn't.

'Sweetie, I know you are still feeling terribly sad and I know you don't want to talk about mum's death, but, well, I thought I'd try to help,' ventured Pops nervously. 'It's a book, you see … The lady at the shop said *you* star in it; it helps you face your fears and challenges. She said it's like being Dorothy in *The Wizard of Oz*, and you loved that when we went to see it at the theatre.' His voice trailed off …

Still feeling confused, she looked at him, love welling in her heart. 'Adorable Pops,' she thought. 'It's not his fault.' 'I'm sorry I yelled. I just always feel confused and don't feel as confident anymore. Go on then. What's the book called?' she said, forcing a smile.

'*You've Got the Power*,' said Pops, with a dramatic punch in the air, which made her laugh. 'It's all about facing challenges and being confident, brilliant and happy.' He smiled, embracing her in a big hug.

'Umm,' she thought, 'I could do with some power if I'm to cope with my mates' new obsession with the school *Strictly* competition, social media, boys and all things make-up …'.

'I'm in, Pops, sign me up. Well, I do like red sparkly shoes …', she giggled as she hugged him.

'Hurray,' said Pops with a big smile.

There we have it. Olivia accepts her call to adventure, and the promise of red sparkly shoes!

Paula thinks:

So many emotions will be spinning around in Olivia's mind, like anger, anxiety, sadness and confusion. It will be a struggle for her to talk about her feelings, especially as her mum was like her best friend, who she would have normally told about her insecurities or feelings of abandonment or worry with friends.

Breath-awareness meditation will help Olivia press pause on her worries and start to relax more. If she does the magic 3 (coming up on day 1) every day, she'll begin to see her emotions settle.

She struggles to talk about her feelings and doesn't want to be seen as different. Her feelings are coming out in anger and frustration because, understandably, they feel so overwhelming and big to deal with. Olivia has experienced a tragedy and feels this sets her apart from everyone. She just wants to fit in. It also appears that it makes everything seem harder because she feels different, and all she really wants is to feel normal again.

She is growing up and it's that time of life when **what her friends think** takes a starring role in her life and influences what she thinks **should be important to her** (even if it's not) – like relationships, make-up and the dance competition. Their expectations are all the harder

for her to cope with because of her bereavement.

Understandably, her world has turned upside down with her mum's death and she feels she is alone facing the feelings of confusion that come with growing up. Gaining an understanding of the mind/body connection over the next few days will also help her understand herself and her emotions more.

You've Got the Power will help Olivia deal with her vulnerability as she grows in courage to face the day-to-day events and challenges life brings. Acceptance of her vulnerability will build her resilience and self-compassion and will support her to open up to her grief, hurt and sadness, and also be open to all the wonderful things in her life.

We'll be checking in on Olivia's ups and downs as she progresses through her hero's journey with you. I said no spoiler alerts – now turn your phone off and let's carry on with the journey.

There are loads of awesome charities and organisations that can help Olivia and Harry, like Mind and Heads Together, who provide invaluable support and helplines. Always ask for help from a family member, teacher or helpline when you are worried.

Check out the list of awesome charities and support groups at the back of the book.

Day 1

Power Breathing

You're busy, right? I feel you – tell me about it: with clubs, homework, Netflix, family and hobbies, who isn't? So, **let's get started with doing nothing.** You might chuckle, but any good hero needs to be relaxed to fire up their **superpower**. The good news is we can plug into our power in just three minutes, and we've all got three minutes no matter how busy we are!

Give this a go – my nickname for it is **magic 3**. It is as simple as this:

⭐ Become aware of your body. Try to sit up straight but don't strain your back and neck, and become aware of what's on your mind, how you are feeling and what sensations you are experiencing in your physical body. Simply accept what is happening in your body in this moment.

⭐ Now bring your attention to your breath – the gentle in and the out. Simply watch the flow of your breath.

⭐ Now bring your attention to any sensations in your body and to the space around your body. Then do nothing! Just breathe for three minutes. You can set the timer on your phone. **Your breath is like an anchor into the present moment; you have a little holiday from worrying about any mistakes you've made in the past or might make in the future.**

How did that feel? Was it easy or hard? Did your mind wander? Mine just did! I just thought of the saying: *yesterday is history, tomorrow is a mystery, but today is a gift.* That's why it's called the **present**.

Power practice: do the magic 3 once a day. It is great for training your brain to be calm.

DAY ONE ☀ POWER POINTS TO REMEMBER

NEVER GIVE UP - WHO KNOWS
WHAT TOMORROW WILL BRING

Consider this statement and then finish the sentence below three times.

∞ I AM OPEN TO CHANGE AND CHALLENGE. ∞

Three small challenges I could give myself for positive change are:

1. _____

2. _____

3. _____

Day 1 affirmation

∞ I have the power: I breathe in calm, I breathe out worry. ∞

😊 Superpower Song for day 1:

🎧 'Don't You Worry 'bout a Thing' by Tori Kelly, ♪
from the movie *Sing*

Day 2

Knowledge Is Power

YOUR AMAZING BRAIN – YES, YOURS!

Yep, your brain is amazing too. I'd hazard a guess that like me you've thought a lot of times, and I mean a lot of times, things like, 'Where is my brain?' or 'Why don't I get it?' I won't be surprised if you're not quite convinced, just yet, that your brain is amazing. But trust me, it is.

Get ready for your first power-light-bulb moment ...

When you get what's going on in your brain, it's a turbo boost in how to make great choices. So, I hear you asking, how? Good question. You know when you are stressed out, feeling overwhelmed, angry or sad, it can be confusing, right? But did you know there's a dead easy way to calm those feelings down? I am guessing no, but don't worry, I am going to tell you how. Even the times when we feel like a failure.

Quick aside ... I guess you already know this timely reminder. Even the great Thomas Edison, Mr Light Bulb himself, said, '**I have not failed**. I've just found 10,000 ways that won't work. Many of life's failures are people who did not realise how close they were to **success** when they gave up.' Edison is clearly an Olympian in **practice makes perfect!**

It's confusing sometimes when our brains become overwhelmed with feelings of fear, sadness or anger. Let's say you've just been asked to read Martin Luther King's 'I Have a Dream' speech in assembly, and you'd rather die! No offence to Dr King, of course ... Instantly your brain will start to go into the stress response. This is when we freak out, feel like running away or are rooted to the spot with anxiety – it happens to us all and it is dead normal.

WARNING! POWER OVERLOAD MAY OCCUR. DO NOT ABORT, I REPEAT, DO NOT ABORT MISSION – SCIENCE STUFF ON ITS WAY ...

Science lets us into the secrets of being awesome, and, by the way, even if you don't love it, it's worth respecting it. Before we get into the science – be patient, it's only a page, two at the most, and I promise it's easy in the end. Let's think about what happens to our brain when we are stressed, possibly when asked to read in assembly. I like the MindUp* model of the brain: it shares the secrets of what it calls the 'three key players' of the brain – the amygdala, prefrontal cortex and hippocampus, very simply – which is pretty cool when we are talking about something so complex!

Catch the video on YouTube for more information, a link is given at the end of week 1. Let's look at what happens to these players in our brain when we become stressed. Stress has three key responses:

Fight – ready for action

Flight – run for the hills

Freeze – rabbit in the headlights

---

*MindUp is a classroom-based social and emotional learning program (SEL) designed to enhance self-awareness, social awareness, attention, self-regulation, problem solving, and pro-social behaviour (helping, sharing, and cooperating).

We get a stress response when our amygdala is triggered – could be just before an exam, or wondering if the muppet who's been known to bully you is up to no good or worrying your parents will go mad because you've just lost one of your £90 trainers. The amygdala jumps to attention as soon as you get stressed – it's the part of the brain which reacts to fear, danger and threat. It is sometimes thought of as the guard dog because it protects us from an actual threat.

The thing is we sometimes exaggerate our problems (we all do), which gets us in a worry tizzy and our guard dog, the amygdala, starts chomping at the bit, aka stressing out a lot. The amygdala helps us deal with our emotions and is particularly aroused when we experience fear or anger as a result of what's going on around us.

This means we literally can't think straight – as useful as a chocolate teapot, as my mum would say! How can we think clearly, I hear you ask? Without a doubt the best way is breathing. I know, it's free and you've been doing it since you were born – what's not to like? Couldn't be easier, hey? Focusing on our breathing helps us calm down and relaxes the idea of the threat. That's why our first hero power was **doing nothing**.

Once we are calm we can access the awesome wizard/ninja part of our brain, the prefrontal cortex. That's probably why people say you should breathe or slowly count to ten to calm down – it helps you think straight. Our old wizard, the prefrontal cortex, is the most evolved part of the brain and it helps us make good decisions. It is also cool for focusing our attention, so we can learn to read, write, decide, predict, intuit, analyse, interpret and get creative with our knowledge.

Professor of psychiatry Dan Siegel uses a cool acronym called FACES to help us remember how the prefrontal cortex helps us be more **f**lexible, **a**daptable, **c**oherent, **e**nergised and **s**table.

Another part of the brain is the hippocampus, and it's all about storage of our memories. It is the part of the brain like a storage vault for all of our memories and learning. It is like a huge computer (subconscious mind) of recordings of everything we have ever seen, sensed, heard or done. If we stay with the idea of a computer, this part of our brain is like when we do a Google search. With our thoughts, we are doing searches all the time and the hippocampus loads information into our conscious mind to help us remember how to face/accept/deal with what's going on in our life.

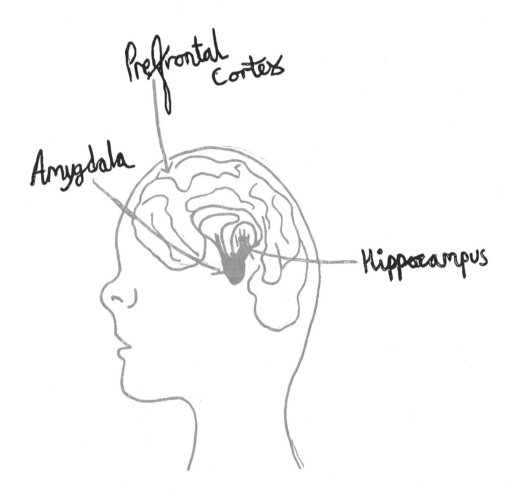

DAY 2: THE BRAVE AND THE BOLD PRIZE GOES TO ...

You must listen to me: the only way to save yourself (and maybe the world) is to **know yourself!** You are powerful beyond measure, but time is a luxury you don't have in decrypting the secrets of X-ray senses. When you know this, it will be like putting a giant force field around yourself that radiates the powerful assurance that **you are not only enough, but awesome too.**

Are you brave and bold enough for this?

Of course you are. When you get to know yourself, miracles happen. Let's start by getting to know how you feel when you are stressed, worried or anxious, etc. Our brain is hardwired to be on the lookout for threats – this was useful in caveman times so we could run away from lions. Not as useful if we're worrying about getting rejected or not feeling enough – our body experiences the same chemical response as it does with the idea that a lion is about to get us, which makes us feel worse! Try this out: think of something a bit stressful, and notice what happens in your body. Write the sensations down. Now think about what you were saying to yourself as you thought of the stress.

**Sensations –
what happens in your body**

1. _____

2. _____

3. _____

4. _____

**Thoughts –
what you tell yourself**

1. _____

2. _____

3. _____

4. _____

Again, we have no time to lose. When we get to know how our body feels (maybe heart beating faster, shallow breathing, funny tummy, shaky hands, bright as a beetroot or wobbly knees, to name a few) we can get good at noticing this stuff and training our brain in ways to manage it.

Did you notice what you said to yourself? Sometimes it's not nice (maybe 'I'm no good,' 'I can't do that,' 'I am so stupid,' 'My friend is funnier than me,' 'My sister is the clever one,' 'Why can't I do it?' 'They'll be so disappointed in me,' 'I'm rubbish at sport' … just a few again!), but don't worry – we're going to learn how to reframe, i.e. change, that stinking thinking in the next few weeks!

Before moving on, do the magic 3 breathing. Close your eyes, it's time to do nothing!

By unanimous vote:
the prize – you are awesome – goes to you!

SPILL THE BEANS ... WHAT'S IN IT FOR ME AND HOW DO I KNOW YOU'RE RIGHT?

Hey, don't just take my word for it – give it try and if you're still not convinced about the superpower of practising awareness and the magic 3, see what our famous guru Google has to say!

The greatest scientific minds across the planet show breath awareness and witnessing our thoughts:

⭐ helps to improve happiness and our sense of well-being

⭐ gives us better focus and concentration

⭐ helps us handle stress, anxiety, doubts and fear

⭐ increases self-awareness and our ability to make good choices

⭐ reduces stress and enhances relaxation

⭐ improves our creativity and sense of contentment

⭐ helps us deal better with tricky situations in our relationships

⭐ increases calm and kind behaviour

⭐ helps us respond better when we feel angry or hurt

⭐ makes us more understanding of others and ourselves.

DAY TWO ☀ POWER POINTS TO REMEMBER

Margaret Mead, an anthropologist who studied how children learn, famously said, 'Children must be taught how to think, not what to think.' I like that – it helps you own your power. You can train your brain to be calmer, more optimistic and have stronger self-belief. Think of the brain as a mental muscle – you can tone it and get it into great shape! We have to take it to the gym, though. You've got to practise.

Consider this statement and then finish the sentence below three times.

MY BEAUTIFUL STRONG MIND

∞ I CAN TRAIN MY BRAIN, I CAN CHOOSE MY THOUGHTS
AND I CREATE WITH MY THOUGHTS. ∞

Three small ways I can train my brain for kinder thinking are:

1. _____

2. _____

3. _____

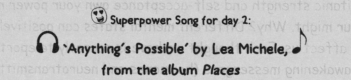

Day 2 affirmation

∞ I am a creator - my words and thoughts create my world.
I breathe in kindness; I breathe out acceptance. ∞

👀 Superpower Song for day 2:

🎧 'Anything's Possible' by Lea Michele, 🎵
from the album *Places*

Day 3

The Mind/Body Connection

So now for the mind-blowing *You've Got the Power* game changer! We can avert catastrophe by using our own power, and restrain worry by how we think, speak and act. **Did you know that where the mind goes the body will follow?** You rule your mind and you alone can rule it. This is an adventure in consciousness – a choice in what you want to create.

Let's take a closer look.

You might be surprised that the mind/body connection happens on both a physical and a chemical level. In this part of the adventure you'll discover the real world of the brain as the vehicle that allows you to experience thoughts, beliefs, attitudes and emotions through your mind. Your mind always does what it thinks you want; it doesn't care if what you say is right or wrong or good or bad, it just acts on your words to manifest what you're thinking.

Your mission is to force worry thinking to loosen its grip on your life, and with titanic strength and self-acceptance own your power mindset with all your might. Why? Different mental states can positively or negatively affect us. Each thought we have is secretly teleporting through the body, awakening messengers (hormones and neurotransmitters) that can either destroy or save our well-being.

I hear you: why the big secret, why keep you in the dark all this time on the one bit of information that could literally transform your life? Crazy. Your imagination rules and you can use your imagination to create great thoughts and transform painful thinking. **Fact.**

Happiness is in the balance. This is one of your most precious superpowers for transformation to take place. Your brain is headquarters but your mind is the boss. If you know your brain you can rewire it. Once you understand this there is no turning back. You don't know your powers yet, but you soon will. This knowledge will help you achieve anything – well, almost anything – if you practise. **Good luck.**

Thinking affects feeling and feeling affects action. That's right – you have a say in your well-being by how you think, act and speak! *You've Got the Power!*

DAY 3: DON'T TAKE MY WORD FOR IT – TEST IT OUT!

How to elicit (bring out) stress: You've got this challenge – we need to do it to show you how your thoughts teleport through your body, activating emotions. Brace yourself: incoming missile. Close your eyes, if that's comfy and safe too. Start by becoming aware of your breathing. If it's fast, make it slower.

Now remember a time that you felt a little stressed – all hope dwindling away as you worried, feeling frustrated or anxious. Can you see what is happening? Do you hear anyone or your own voice? How does it feel? What's happening? What can you see and hear? With your X-ray senses notice where you feel stressed or ruffled in your body. Take a few more breaths then open your eyes.

Can you believe just remembering stress makes you feel as weirded out as you did when it happened? That's another thing about the brain – it can't tell the difference between what's real (**actually happening**) and what's unreal (**happening in our imagination**). It gives you emotions to match your thinking. The more you worry, the worse you feel – trapping yourself in a loop of thinking and feeling that doesn't help you at all.

The funny thing about feelings is they hang around, and I bet you're still feeling a bit off, so let's change that. Now close your eyes and be aware of your breathing – the gentle in and out. Remember a time that you felt really good. Can you see what is making you feel so happy? Are you laughing with your mates or smashing the winning goal? Does it feel warm and joyful? Maybe turn up the brightness on your pleasant thoughts – see how you can increase your happy hormones just by using your mind? Take a few more breaths, breathing in your happy thoughts, then open your eyes.

Phew. That's better. These experiments show us we can activate stress or happiness by how we think, speak and act. You might feel stress before taking a test or giving a class presentation, facing a tough opponent in a sport or dancing in front of friends at a party. These situations are hardly life-or-death – it's just your nervous system responding to help you perform well under pressure. When it happens, you can use your thoughts to help you rise to a challenge and meet it with alertness, focus and strength. Facing these challenges, rather than backing away from them, is a part of learning and growing.

As I said, the brain is like a muscle and that's why neuro scientists tell us as muscle grows when we exercise the body, so do parts of the brain when we exercise them with different thinking or meditating; they call this neuroplasticity. Excitement and fear feel the same but the meaning we give them determines how we respond. If you're happy to speak up in class you'll feel excitement: if you're afraid you'll be judged then you'll feel fear.

I CHOOSE: I AM THE CREATOR: I FREE MY MIND

Consider this statement and then finish the sentence below three times:

∞ I CAN CHOOSE WHAT I THINK. WHAT I CHOOSE STRENGTHENS MY ABILITY TO FEEL IT MORE. I CHOOSE KINDNESS OVER FEAR. ∞

Three ways I can train my brain for more 'feel-good' muscles are:

1. _____

2. _____

3. _____

Day 3 affirmation

∞ **I create with kindness. I breathe in kindness; I breathe out calmness.** ∞

😊 **Superpower Song for day 3:**

🎧 **'The Circle of Life' by Carmen Twillie and Lebo M.,** ♪
from the movie *The Lion King*

Day 4

Power Chemicals in the Body

In your biggest or even smallest victories, your brain naturally creates chemicals, like endorphins, that make you feel even better and more able to face unexpected stress and worry. These body chemicals help you face dilemmas and problems. When we feel under threat, our thoughts and feelings can make us feel jittery and we release stress chemicals, like cortisol. These chemicals can help you with noble and heroic acts as you avert danger.

Stress chemicals are only trying to protect us in dangerous situations and they could save our lives. The trouble is we release them when we are not really in danger, eroding our well-being and making us feel anxious and afraid. When we capture these essential truths about the human body we can use them to our advantage.

Let's take a closer look at these two key characters, also known as neuro transmitters, which are important chemicals that we can recruit as our allies and not our deadliest foes in the quest for greater happiness, confidence and joy.

Cortisol is a fear chemical and it can become your most dangerous enemy when overactivated. It is needed for the fight-or-flight response when you are in danger. When we over-worry, exaggerate or gossip we can release cortisol into our system when it is not needed, which basically makes us feel rubbish because it decreases the hormones that make us feel happy.

Endorphins are happy hormones that are released when we feel good. Like hugging our parents, achieving something we want, playing with our dog or having ice cream on the beach. Endorphins are ace – they are your miracle hormone, they help reduce pain in your body, and are responsible for sensations of pleasure and the euphoria of great achievement.

Where the mind goes the body follows: using your X-ray sense of awareness is being mindful. Being mindful is all about smart thinking, and you don't have to be top of the class for that. It's all about being aware of how and what you think, do and say to yourself or others will make you feel. That is, happy or sad.

Get into the great habit of asking, 'Will this behaviour make me feel better or worse?' It doesn't take a genius to make brilliant, intelligent, smart choices now, does it?

TURNING ON THE BODY'S NATURAL POWER

The truth is **you've got the power to identify, accept and improve how you feel**. Have a look through the list below and check out where you can moderate your behaviour. Trying for 80/20 is always a good approach. We might not get things right all the time – I mean, who does? But being mindful (being aware of what is happening in the present moment) will help us make some happy hormone choices that feel good, and being mindful can help us avoid actions that could end up making us feel bad.

Mindfulness is about being aware – e.g., I have stage fright and this is how it feels (anxious), or I enjoy singing and this is how it feels (wonderful).

Increasing endorphins	Increasing cortisol
Believing you are enough	Feeling unworthy
Having a laugh	Tension, feeling stressed out
Deep sleep	Disturbed sleeping
Positive thinking	Negative thinking
Being playful and curious	Can't be bothered, disinterested
Goals and purpose	Apathy
Friends, sharing with your mates	Loneliness and avoiding people
Sunshine	No sunshine
Meditation and mindfulness	Boredom and worry
Deep breathing	Shallow breathing
Good-mood food	Some processed foods
Letting go of painful events	Mean thinking, gossiping
Plenty of fresh water	Fizzy drinks, coke, etc.
Relaxation	Frustration
Connecting	Feeling lonely
Feeling good about yourself	Rejecting yourself
Fresh air	Ventilated air
Exercise	Lack of exercise

Choose a winning life with loving
thoughts and actions.

DAY FOUR ☼ POWER POINTS TO REMEMBER

As Spider-Man's grandad advised, 'With great power comes great responsibility!' In a nutshell, your responsibility is to accept you create your world with your thoughts. Once you get that **where the mind goes the body follows**, you understand that you need to care for yourself by not worrying too much about painful, stressful emotions, and by opening your awareness to what feels good in life.

Consider this statement and then finish the sentence below three times:

∞ WHEN I WORRY TOO MUCH, I CREATE STRESS
CHEMICALS WHICH CAN MAKE ME FEEL ANXIOUS.
I CHOOSE TO CREATE RELAXATION. ∞

I accept we all worry and I believe three ways I can train my brain to create more relaxation and therefore more 'feel-good' muscles are:

1. _____

2. _____

3. _____

I CHOOSE

Day 5

No Biggie – Just Transformation – What if It Is Not for Me?

First things first, what do I mean by 'just transformation'? 'Hang on,' I hear you say, 'I'm not sure I'm ready for this adventure – call the emergency services, name your price. I want to stay in my own world.' I get it, it's way beyond your comfort zone, but stay with me. New stuff is always a bit scary, but that's part of the fun! You're the boss of your brain. Come on – own it.

Whatever you want to be brilliant at, I am here to help you. Well, that's not strictly true, but the book you are holding is. The thing is no matter how much you resist or how far you run, you can't outrun yourself! Knowing this puts the finishing touches to your greatness and making it happen is at hand – we have no time to lose.

I know lots of anxieties and worries can hold you back, but you've got this, you're on fire and ready to light the launch pad to your power mindset. You have the power to develop your abilities and intelligence to support what you want to achieve. The greatest minds across the planet have congregated to confirm that our beliefs have a great impact on our achievement. Imagination rules, and our attitude preps us for unlimited potential.

ATTITUDES OF THE POWER MINDSET

Check this out – it is amazing. The **seven wonders of the mind**:

1. Accepting 'what is'

2. Embracing your uniqueness

3. Being grateful

4. Knowing what you want

5. Realising anything is possible – your potential is infinite

6. Being mindful and compassionate

7. Knowing we are all connected.

TELL ME MORE. HOW DO I GET THE POWER MINDSET?

Listen, you're at a crossroads in your journey of **who you want to be and who you are**, and attention is crucial for success to be assured. Go easy on yourself – everyone was a baby once, and that includes your favourite film star, singer, sportswoman, footballer or astronaut! Successful people don't just get successful overnight. They have to work hard and practise their power. Adopting this **power mindset** will make what you felt impossible easily achievable. I know, it's brilliant, isn't it? Ready? Then let's begin.

1. Accepting what is: All of our suffering is caused by getting what we didn't want and not getting what we wanted. Acceptance helps us tap into our power. The still place of power inside us, alive with creativity, peace and joy, is awesome. Did you know the average person has about 60 to 80,000 thoughts per day? Albeit unconsciously, all happening in the background. Time to control your thinking instead of it controlling you. You've got the power, and it is a choice.

2. Embracing your uniqueness: You are awesome! You have a special talent – even if you've not found it yet, you have one. Trust me, I know. **You have a superpower and your signature talent will be as unique as your fingerprint.**

3. Being grateful: It feels good when we are grateful, right? Do you have an attitude of gratitude? Gratitude is about focusing on the good and being thankful for the things we have – it increases our happy hormones and it reduces stress levels. Gratitude is the injection of power our heart needs to stay healthy and happy!

4. Knowing what you want: If you don't know what you want, how can you get it? Be clear about how you want to think, feel and be. What do you want to achieve in the next week, month, six months, year or even life? Visualise your goals and dreams.

5. Realising anything is possible: Sure, nobody is perfect but don't limit yourself. If you keep learning from your mistakes, and there will be plenty of them, you'll get your 'light-bulb' moment. Mistakes are opportunities in the adventure of infinite possibility that is your life.

6. Being mindful and compassionate: In other words, be aware and kind in how you think, speak and act. You are the main character and the world is your stage. Be the best version of you. Do the right thing, be generous, be happy for others, and be kind to yourself and others.

7. Knowing we are all connected: Just think of all the people it took to build your house or school, or the epic chain of events it took to provide your breakfast or your favourite clothes. Trees help us breathe, the earth feeds us – nature is awesome. It has the same creative intelligence in it that created you and me. We are of equal value, every contribution we make to the world around us can help it grow. Think about how to make the planet more sustainable for the future kids on it, or even your kids! Too weird? OK, let's continue.

Wonder power

DAY 5: POWERFUL CHOICES FOR ME, MYSELF AND I

Do the magic 3, then put your thinking cap on and have a go at the following.

Write down three of the seven wonders of the mind that you rock at, with examples:

1. _____

2. _____

3. _____

Three wonders you'd like to improve upon and why:

1. _____

2. _____

3. _____

Three wonder powers you want to get a handle on and really create a new habit of living them:

1. _____

2. _____

3. _____

Thinking wonderfully feels wonderful

Game: 'I believe you should give 100% on the court, so I chase every ball.'—Andy Murray

Set: 'I really think a champion is defined not by their wins but by how they can recover when they fail.'—Serena Williams

Match: Andy Murray is the reigning Olympic champion, having won twice. He has won 3 grand-slam tournaments and lost 8, won 14 Masters 1000 series and lost 7, to share just a little of his career. Murray has won over 58 million US dollars in prize money.

Serena Williams has won 23 grand-slam tournaments and lost 8. She has won the gold in the Olympics once in singles and three times in doubles. Earning almost 29 million US dollars in prize money and endorsements, Williams was the highest-paid female athlete in 2016.

Murray and Williams have had loads of great career highs *and* lows (the above is just a snippet), and they didn't give up! They kept practising.

Power reminder: accept that highs and lows are a part of life, and they too shall pass!

DAY FIVE ☀ POWER POINTS TO REMEMBER

By now you are really getting the message that **what you think about comes about**, and experience is teaching you that **you reap what you sow**. You can sow seeds (actions and thoughts) of love and kindness through the process of neuroplasticity – i.e., change the structure of your brain to reap more of what you want in life, like kindness, joy, happiness, patience, fun: it's your choice.

I GROW MY BRAIN WITH COMPASSION AND AWARENESS

Consider this statement and then finish the sentence below three times.

∞ WHEN I THINK WITH COMPASSION AND AWARENESS,
I BECOME MORE COMPASSIONATE AND AWARE.
I CHOOSE MY THOUGHTS. ∞

Three ways I can train my brain to be more compassionate and aware are:

1. _____

2. _____

3. _____

Day 5 affirmation

∞ I create with compassion. I breathe in compassion;
I breathe out awareness. ∞

😺 Superpower Song for day 5:

🎧 'Can't Stop the Feeling' by Justin Timberlake, ♪
from the movie *Trolls*

Day 6

Ditching Worry

First, a few facts. Sometimes you may wreak havoc on your life and sometimes others hurt your feelings, maybe even bully you, and you are easily bruised. You can be strong or sad, spoilt or a pleaser, needy or the leader, and still sometimes people will twist your words into lies to serve their purposes. This stuff happens. The worst thing is that it makes it easier for your thoughts to lead your quest into disaster, asking the universal question, '**Am I enough?**'

Listen, it really isn't fair when people hurt you, but it would be even worse if you then hurt yourself even more by firing shots of criticism at yourself as though you are the enemy. Sometimes we make these trials harder than they need to be with our thinking. I get it – it can be really hard to remember your brilliance when you are troubled. The seven worries of the world, given a chance, will launch their attack when your defences are low and try to make you refuse your call to adventure – don't let them. You are a hero!

Here are the key villains that can have a cataclysmic impact on your mind at any given time. Go with caution, they are highly dangerous and can diminish your power and your light.

Check this out, it's awful. The **seven worries of the world**:

1. Fighting with reality

2. I am not good enough

3. I can't ask for help

4. Worrying about the past

5. I need to control the future

6. Running on FEAR – **f**alse **e**vidence **a**ppearing **r**eal

7. I am not as good as them.

DITCHING THE WORRY MINDSET

Now, what do these awful worries really mean for me?

1. Fighting with reality – you can't accept 'what is'. OK, this is really tricky and we all do it. It boils down to not getting what we want and getting what we didn't want. 'I wanted to go to X's party and I didn't want those shoes mum bought me, they are a show!' 'I needed the county time in backstroke, not butterfly, for the Nationals!'

2. I am not enough – feeling low self-worth and not valuing yourself diminishes your well-being. The worry mindset will always be asking the big fear-building question, 'Am I enough? Like 'I'm no good at that – everyone is better than me.' Really, is that true? 'If only I had green eyes or could sing! X has both – it's just not fair.' 'I give up! It's just too hard, why can't I do better?' 'I'll never be able to be as good as ...'

3. I can't ask for help – or you're too cool to admit you made mistakes. 'I don't want people to know I make mistakes, they'll think I'm a loser.' 'Even if it means I feel bad for sharing a stupid Instagram or Snapchat message that made someone else feel bad, I might pretend I don't.' 'I certainly won't ask for help as I might look weak.' 'I don't want to look stupid.'

4. Worrying about the past – 'Will I ever be enough/get it right?' 'The truth is I am really bad at sport, why should I try?' I don't like getting mocked because Mr or Miss Star Player always sneer at me when I mess up.' 'Anyway, that feels bad – I am going to avoid it. I mean, what happens if I try and get it wrong? The shame. No, never again.'

5. I need to control the future. 'I will only be happy if I go to the dance with X or I get an A grade in art or win a scholarship at ballet.' 'If I can't go to senior school with my mates I will hate my life, I won't be happy.' 'If I don't get the exam results I need my parents will go mad, my teachers will think I can't cut it.' 'No, I will only be happy if everything goes the way I want it to! I need to control it all.'

6. Running on FEAR – **false evidence appearing real.** Just because you tell yourself all of the above is true, that doesn't mean it is. **Thoughts are not facts.** If a friend doesn't respond instantly to our text and we are having a good day we think they must be busy or they have choir practice, but if we are feeling vulnerable we think, 'What did I do wrong?' 'I'm worthless.' 'I knew it, nobody likes me!'

7. I am not as good as them – not trusting that you, like everybody else on the planet, have inner power, and that we are all equal. When we undervalue ourselves or our experience it feels horrible. Winston Churchill once said, 'Courage is what it takes to stand up and speak and courage is also what it takes to sit down and listen.' Make time to listen to your heart, and trust in your dreams. Focusing on your flaws feels bad; using powerful, positive words feels good – the choice is yours; you are valued and valuable!

INSTEAD OF:

TRY:

Fighting with Reality
I am not enough
I can't Ask for help
Worrying about the past
I need to control the future
Running on FEAR:
False Evidence Appearing Real
I'm not as good as them

① Accepting 'what is'
② Embracing your Uniqueness
③ Being Grateful
④ Knowing what you want
⑤ Anything is possible
⑥ Being mindful and Compassionate
⑦ Seeing we are all connected

---

*Follow your bliss and the universe
will open doors for you where
there were only walls.*

—Joseph Campbell

DAY 6: POWERFUL CHOICES FOR ME, MYSELF AND I

Do the magic 3. Now put on your thinking cap and have a go at the following.

Write down three of the seven worries of the world that affect you most, with examples:

1. _____

2. _____

3. _____

Three worries you'd like to ditch, and why:

1. _____

2. _____

3. _____

Three that diminish your power but you're not sure how to break the habit of thinking them:

1. _____

2. _____

3. _____

A common saying in the training world is, 'If you always do what you've always done, you'll always get what you've always got!'

We tend to like things our own way, which is why all of our suffering is caused by not getting what we wanted and getting what we didn't want! That means we fight with reality. The antidote to this is accepting 'what is'. Once a thing has happened, often we can't change it, and if we don't like it, it's no use worrying about it or getting angry as it doesn't help. In the trade we call that 'suffering over our suffering'.

I ACCEPT THAT LIFE HAS ITS UPS AND DOWNS

Consider this statement and then finish the following sentence three times.

∞ I ACCEPT LIFE HAS ITS UPS AND DOWNS.
I RECOGNISE FIGHTING WITH REALITY CREATES
MORE STRESS, HURT, ANGER, JEALOUSY OR PAIN.
I CHOOSE ACCEPTANCE OVER FEAR. ∞

Three ways I can train my brain for more 'feel-good' muscles are:

1. _____

2. _____

3. _____

Day 6 affirmation

∞ I accept myself; when I get down, I get up again.
I breathe in self-love; I breathe out trust. ∞

😺 Superpower Song for day 6:

🎧 'Get Back Up Again' by Anna Kendrick, ♪
from the movie *Trolls*

Day 7

Power Choice – Making the Power-Mindset Shift

How's it going? It's tough navigating your story, I know. You're just a girl/guy with a dream, who went after it, giving it everything you've got along the way, and dealing with the stuff that has been thrown at you on our adventure so far. It's usually around this point you're wondering, 'How did I get myself into this?' 'Can I really pull it off?' 'Get me out of the line of fire.' 'Enough.' 'Nope, negative, I am not playing.'

I get it – you've identified your worries and you don't like it. But take heart, help is on the way. We can contain our worries and here's a great way. Let's create a worry jar, or what I like to think of as an 'is-it-true? jar'.

Potential worries that you could place in your jar:

⭐ **'Everyone is better than me.'** Really, is that true? Come on, you are definitely better at some things.

⭐ **'Nope I can't do it.'** Would you be willing to try a little part of it?

⭐ **'I'll never be able to join the dance group.'** Or have you just not had enough practice yet to try out for it?

⭐ **'I give up on things.'** Would you be open to sticking with one thing to prove you can?

We have a heart on our worry jar because it is much harder to motivate ourselves to change when we speak meanly to ourselves. Remember, we create endorphins or cortisol by how we think, act and speak. Staying kind and calm helps us be more resilient. Sure, I know it takes courage because you have to take action, usually to prove you can! But you can with the power mindset. You may need to get help, but all great people ask for help. You may need to practise more but, again, all successful people practise.

Think of some of the things/thoughts that worry you or hold you back from trying out new things (refer to yesterday's list). Now write them down on slips of paper and pop them in the jar. Let's move from worrier to warrior by asking, 'Are my worries really true?' Think of one or two things you can do in the coming week to challenge your worries.

The greatest minds across the planet have found writing your worries down and placing them safely in a jar helps you stop worrying so much. The other cool thing is once a week, in the morning (not a great idea to do this just before bed), you can look at your worries and decide if they are still true. Some will be, and some won't be. You'll add new ones and take old ones away. You can throw away the ones that don't worry you any more, and if some still feel too tricky maybe you'd like to have a chat with a friend, teacher or relative to help you feel better.

DAY 7: THE POWER OF STILLNESS IN YOU

Start out with your magic 3.

Now imagine a lake, a huge, deep blue lake. The weather is constantly changing, just like our thoughts. On calm, sunny days the surface of the lake will be glassy and still, and reflect the passing clouds, but when there are storms, wind and rain, the water will be agitated, muddy and turbulent. Do you accept your thoughts are just like the weather?

Even the bed of the lake may have old boots and bottles on, rubbish no longer needed, just sitting there waiting to be cleared away. Beneath the rubbish the surface is solid and still; if you go down deep enough, there is always calm, a beautiful untouchable stillness. Beneath everything we can feel a presence of love inside of us.

This lake is you, or, rather, your mind. The weather is the events in your life and the surface of the water is your thoughts and emotions. Maybe the rubbish is the mistakes you made ages ago and you still haven't let yourself off the hook for them. I know you get scared, but no matter what is happening on the surface remember to anchor yourself, let go and stop attaching to the past. Just get a little kinder with yourself.

There is a deep place you can go to where there is always peace, calm and stillness. A place that feels like home, a place of safety and contentment. In this space the past and future fade – no labels, no worries, just being. It is the presence of the power of love in your heart. It's what Buddha, Jesus and Mohammed talked about, but it's not religious – it's your spirit. You have mind, body, emotions and spirit. Your spirit helps you find bliss in your mind, body and emotions. It's pretty cool and it's the powerful essence of your being.

This is called mindful meditation and, like breath awareness, it gives you a sense of calm and more clarity, and it reminds you of the still power within you.

How was it? I bet you wanted to open your eyes. Keeping them closed helps you relax more, though. This exercise helps you settle your mind and become more aware and open in the present moment. It is mad that we can feel peace inside, in any moment, even when everything outside seems crazy, worrying and busy. Write any reflections down in your journal and be open to insight. Think about how the spirit of kindness connects us and the spirit of fear separates us from one another.

You are braver than you believe,

stronger than you seem,

and smarter than you think.

—A.A. Milne, *Winnie-the-Pooh*

Mindfulness can be practised anytime, anywhere, by noticing what our mind is doing and gently bringing ourselves back to the present moment. It is very likely that your mind will drift off repeatedly. That is to be expected. Mindfulness helps you slow down, it gives you a second to breathe and choose your response instead of acting without thinking on what we call autopilot. When we slip into autopilot, our attention is absorbed in our wandering minds and we are not really 'present' in our own lives.

MIND-FUll   MINDFUL

MINDFULNESS SLOWS BUSY THOUGHTS DOWN AND CLEARS MY MIND

Consider this statement and then finish the following sentence three times.

∞ WHEN I AM MINDFUL, I AM AWARE OF MY THOUGHTS, SPEECH AND ACTIONS. MINDFULNESS STRENGTHENS MY ABILITY TO BE PRESENT AND CHOOSE WITH POWER. ∞

Three ways I can train my brain to be more mindful are:

1. _____

2. _____

3. _____

Day 7 affirmation

∞ Breathing in I am aware of my breath; breathing out I smile at my breath. ∞

😊 Superpower Song for day 7:

🎧 'The Power of Yet', by C. J. Luckey, from the album C.A.P.S. ♪

😊 Week 1 inspiration:

Martha explains the MindUp brain model on YouTube -:
https://youtu.be/XDppZOeWLR0

WEEK TWO

CHANGING YOUR VIEW OF THE WORLD

ACT ONE – STILL IN THE SEPARATION PHASE

- ✔ Rejecting the invitation
- ✔ Trusting your mentor

---

*In order to carry out a positive action
we must develop a positive vision.*

—Nelson Mandela

Day 8

Getting the Power Mindset

The world would be a boring place if we were all the same. Thank goodness we are not. Life is about being the best you can be. There's an old saying, 'Greatness isn't born. It's grown'! As we found out earlier, we've got a big say in how our greatness is grown and when we own that – the sky's the limit! You are one of 7.6 billion (and counting) people in the world and you're fabulously, brilliantly, amazingly as unique as can be. When we embrace our uniqueness we don't have to compare ourselves with others any more. Phew, that's a relief!

Go big or go home! OK, it's time. Drum roll please ...

Every great hero's journey begins somewhere. Remember, Harry Potter's did in the *Philosopher's Stone*, when he got his 'letter from no one'. And yours did here, with your mission back in the section 'Welcome to Your New Powerful Life!' in 'Week One'.

This adventure of self-discovery has taken us out of the sameness of the 'I worry' ordinary world, and called us on a tricky journey of personal responsibility. Oh yes, we spotted all those bits of us we don't like and had to love them anyway, because that's what powerful people do! Don't worry, even Harry Potter wasn't sure he was up for the task – telling Hagrid, 'I think you must have made a mistake. I don't think I can be a wizard.'

You bet, just like Harry Potter, we've resisted sometimes kicking and screaming. I know you've got a lot on your plate and it's a miracle you get out of bed some days, let alone transform yourself and the world. Remember, greatness isn't born – it is grown. But wasn't it fantastic when you committed to the adventure and realised your superpowers? Wasn't it brilliant when you empowered yourself magically, manifesting good feelings? OK, so not the traditional invisibility cloak, but **you've got the power** is invisible to the naked eye too, although in fairness it does shine out of you, for all to see!

You, my friend, are growing into my type of greatness. You are our centre-stage, real live hero, brandishing your powerful thoughts with stealth and skill. I know you will have been tested! The enemy 'I worry' will have launched a few attacks and mostly been defeated by your **I've-got-the-power** thinking.

STUFF HAPPENS – HAPPY STUFF, SAD STUFF AND DON'T-CARE STUFF

In the trade we describe stuff happening as pleasant–unpleasant–neutral events. The idea is it's unrealistic to think you'll always be deliriously happy because stuff happens. All these states have one thing in common. *They will pass.* You know this, even in the last few days we've experienced it. You can declare without hesitation, '**This too shall pass.**'

On this adventure you are gathering the tools with which to live by this. Living this truth helps you create an unyielding compassion for yourself. As a hero of thought you blow open your biggest enemy, worry, with acceptance of what is, quit living in the future and stop fretting over the past. It helps you face the situation at hand. Even when it's not your finest hour you'll take courage in the knowledge that **this too shall pass**.

Basically, it offers hope. Life is everchanging and stuff happens – the trick is not to let the stuff define us. The snippet of story below shows this:

A king once asked a wise man to help him find peace. Desperate to know, he asked, 'Is there a mantra that works in every situation in every place and every time? It has to work when you are happy or when you are sad; in every defeat and every victory.' The king wanted one answer for all questions. Finally, the wise man, after some time, gave the king a beautiful ring with the inscription, 'This too shall pass' ...

Stuff in life can hurt and confuse us or make us feel clear and happy. The trick is not to be too critical with yourself. We are all learning. You wouldn't say to a baby trying to learn to walk, when it fell down, 'Oh, you're rubbish. You're no good at that. Don't ever try walking again!' Our mind labels stuff 'good' or 'bad' and then our brain teleports signals through the body getting us ready to relax or get stressed. Remember, we are not our suffering - we experience sadness or happiness and they are just part of life. Remember, **you've got the power** and **this too shall pass.**

DAY EIGHT ☀ POWER POINTS TO REMEMBER

Here today, gone tomorrow. We know everything in life passes – that is the nature of things. Look how much you've changed since you were a baby. Fashions and fads change, just as friendships and hobbies do. We change and grow all the time; things we once loved we grow bored of, as our interests expand or we dedicate ourselves to one particular passion.

Consider this statement and then finish the sentence below three times:

∞ EVERYTHING CHANGES; I ACCEPT LIFE IS ALWAYS CHANGING. I CHOOSE TO GO WITH THE FLOW. ∞

Three ways I can stop resisting change and go with the flow are:

1. _____

2. _____

3. _____

I think a hero is an ordinary individual who
finds strength to persevere and endure
in spite of overwhelming obstacles.

—Superman

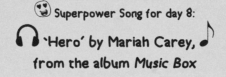

Day 8 affirmation

∞ **Life is always changing. I breathe in acceptance; I breathe out calm.** ∞

😊 **Superpower Song for day 8:**
🎧 'Hero' by Mariah Carey, ♪
from the album *Music Box*

Day 9

Confidence Is Like a Muscle

In coaching, we think of confidence as a **muscle you can grow** and you'd be amazed at the number of times you get to flex your confidence muscle throughout your day. If you don't think of yourself as confident, that's okay – you can act 'as if' and gradually you'll feel more confident. Building our confidence helps us to stay with the adventure, even when we are tempted to reject our call and stay in the 'same old world of worry'.

Keep in mind that while practice creates competence, to have the confidence to get going you have to believe you can achieve. Make sure you don't give your power away by basing it on other people or things. Your power and confidence flow from inside you, so it's important to have your own back.

SIX SIMPLE STRATEGIES FOR BUILDING SELF-CONFIDENCE

You can use these strategies to help build up, tune, and improve your self-confidence. They will also grow your 'I believe in myself' neuropathways, aka brain muscles.

1. Practise your dream; as always, practice makes perfect – or at least much better. Practice is the attitudinal muscle of success.

2. Behave as if you are more confident than you are – the 'fake it till you make it' strategy. It's like trying on your dream for size.

3. Be flexible, try to relax and let go of judging yourself.

4. Learn from your mistakes – remember Mr Light Bulb? It's important to keep on keeping on. Jim Carrey shares, '**You can fail at what you don't want, so you might as well take a chance on doing what you love.**'

5. Silence your inner critic – the voice of self-blame and attack feels awful and fills you with low-mood chemicals. Yuck, why would you?

6. Be kind to yourself – the side effects feel beautiful!

DAY 9: FLICK THE CONFIDENCE SWITCH

Power exercise: 10 minutes

Remember a time you felt really confident, or imagine one that will make you feel confident.

Now imagine this confident memory/thought as a movie screen and you are in the movie – see yourself larger than life right there on the screen. Using your imagination, continue to visualise what you saw, heard and felt, and really connect with how good it was. Who is there? Are you laughing? Where are you? What are the sounds and smells?

See the screen of 'your life' really bright with vivid colours. What can you hear? As you think about the memory, turn up the sound and the brightness on your screen.

To help you remember this really confident time you can create a little reminder. Try squeezing your thumb and second finger together on your right hand as you think about your confident memory. This squeezing action can become a new trigger to bring back your confident memory. A bit like a magic power button – or a confidence switch.

This way, the next time you are feeling unsure, anxious or nervous, just squeeze your thumb and second finger and remember your confident memory. This is your confidence switch, and every time you use it you are creating confidence muscles in your brain.

When you are in a situation where you have performance anxiety, take a breath and 'view' it. This can help you see more clearly what's going on. Imagine you are watching a play and you are one of the actors – it might help you see what's going on for the other characters too. Check out the type of role you are playing. Are you demonstrating all the practice and hard work you've put in by how you are behaving? Maybe without the nerves your confidence could shine?

Remember, stress kicks off the amygdala and prevents you accessing your prefrontal cortex, the part that helps with good reasoning ability. When the amygdala is alert you also can't reach the stored learning in your hippocampus, so it makes sense to do the magic 3 and flick your confidence switch whenever you are getting ready for exams.

DAY NINE ☀ POWER POINTS TO REMEMBER

Listen, we can't be confident all the time, because we are always learning and growing, and it takes time to build new skills. That said, you also have to be open to being awesome at your chosen passion. Whether a dancer, writer, scientist, swimmer or runner, doing just enough to get by won't cut it. Following your heart inspires you to give of your best, and that means more of a challenge as it takes more practice and courage to do your best.

FOLLOW YOUR HEART - IT KNOWS THE WAY

Consider this statement and then finish the sentence below three times:

∞ I TRUST IN MYSELF. WHETHER I THINK I CAN OR I THINK I CAN'T,
I AM USUALLY RIGHT, BECAUSE I AM THE CREATOR OF MY LIFE.
I CHANGE CAN'T FOR CAN AND OPEN MY HEART TO MY DREAMS. ∞

Three ways I can follow my heart and build my confidence are:

1. _____

2. _____

3. _____

---

*The privilege of a lifetime
is being who you are.*

—Joseph Campbell

WEEK TWO: TEMPTATION TO REFUSE THE CALL ...

Harry blasted out of his classroom, down the corridor and through the school gate. He'd made it out just in time. In the distance he heard Snake the enemy snarling, 'Harry's in for it today, it will be hilarious.'

He kept running, thinking, 'What will be hilarious? What will they do to me next? Gawd, I hate my life. What's wrong with me? Why do they think they can do this to me?'

He burst in through his front door. 'I'm sweating like a pig,' he thought. 'Some Jedi – the only force leaking out of me is stress!'

'Harry, is that you, love?' His mum called.

'Yeah,' he mumbled.

'Look at you, you're dripping in sweat,' she said, her eyebrows arching with real worry. 'What is it love? What's happened? You look terrified.'

'Don't be daft, mum, I just fancied a run,' he blurted out.

'But you hate running,' she said, sceptically.

'Yeah, well, I've changed my mind. I love it now,' he lied.

'That's brilliant, Harry. I've just got the new term's school-clubs list – I'll sign you up to the running club,' she gushed, excitedly. 'That's lucky, you were only saying last week you should join a club.' She beamed. 'Just great. I'll get on it. Let's make sure you get a space.'

'Hell. How on earth am I going to get out of this?' he thought, drudging up the stairs, throwing himself on his bed. He wondered, and not for the first time, why Snake picked on him. As he lay there, he noticed he was breathing the magic 3 and feeling calmer. Then he started to imagine himself as a real-life Jedi.

In his vision, he was strong in the face of adversity. He placed an impregnable field of power around himself. It felt good. Snake entered the scene and Harry used the force to suspend him in the air. 'Let me down, Harry! Please don't drop me – I promise never to do it again,' pleaded Snake.

'Luckily for you, Snake, it is not the Jedi way to attack.' With an air of newfound confidence he added, in the words of Jedi master Yoda, *'A Jedi uses the Force for knowledge and defence, never for attack.'*

Smiling to himself, he said out loud, 'The Force will always be with you, Harry. Always!'

A little voice in the back of his head started to crack holes in his temporary happiness, with thoughts like, 'Errh, right, as if you could stand up to Snake. Power or no power you can't do it; you'll never be able to stand up to him in real life – you're useless.'

'STOP!' he screamed in his head. 'I've got to try it – anything is better than this hiding away. I might even ask Tom to join the running club too. What was it the book said? ... Connection is a big part of the power mindset. Not only that – a bit of safety in numbers can't hurt.'

Paula thinks:

Understandably, Harry is anxious – it takes a huge amount of courage to stand up to his fears and to a bully. He will worry, 'What if I fail?' but he'll never know unless he tries. We can also see he doesn't want to admit anything is wrong or that he needs help, avoiding telling his mum, even telling fibs – Harry is definitely fighting with reality here.

When Harry starts to adopt the power mindset of the seven wonders of the world, and understands how the seven-worries-of-the-world mindset weakens our resolve and then impacts our feelings through the mind/body connection, this will help him get to grips with how his thinking can make him feel unresourceful and unable to face his fears.

Harry wants to kick his fears into touch and live without the nagging worry of Snake, but it might be easier just to stay in his room. He's stuck between running on FEAR (false evidence appearing real) and accepting he's got the power. He's also a bit bored of avoiding his mates and even decides to ask Tom to join the running club with him, which is a fantastic step in the right direction.

Let's not forget there are going to be lots of thoughts and emotions around his mum and dad's divorce whizzing through his body, creating havoc or hope. I think learning to flick the confidence switch and practising this daily will really build up his resilience.

He is playing with creating a reality, in his imagination as a Jedi, where he is more confident and in control, and this will really empower him and begin to improve his feelings of self-worth and happiness.

Expect a few wobbles yourself as you face up to the challenges of your hero's journey. The temptation to refuse the call happens, don't worry. Keep reading – you've got this and the **power**.

MEANWHILE, OLIVIA IS FINDING LIFE TRICKY TOO ...

'What? How dare she?' Katie exclaimed. 'Don't cry. She's just jealous.'

'Of what?' snivelled Olivia. 'Didn't you hear me? She shouted across the hall in rehearsal that I've got frizzy hair and spots. And I looked ugly with my braces!' spat Oliva, feeling hurt. 'I hate my life. I can never go back to school.'

Katie leaned over and gave her a big hug. 'Your hair is lovely – it's wavy, and your teeth will be beautiful too. Amber has done nothing but create drama since she stopped hanging out with us. She doesn't like that we are so close.'

'I don't care. I never want to see her, ever, ever again! And I miss mum ...,' screamed Olivia.

'Ignore her, lovely Livy. I'm sorry about your mum,' said Katie.

'Please, Katie, I don't want to talk about mum,' said Olivia, looking sad and confused.

'OK, we don't have to. Look, we've been looking forward to doing the school's *Strictly Come Dancing* competition, and she's not going to stop our cha-cha-cha!' Katie exclaimed as she jumped up, doing a few moves from the show.

Olivia was thinking 'I'd rather die than dance in front of everyone. But maybe I can, I love dancing – anything is possible.'

Katie pulled Olivia up off her bed. 'Let's cha-cha-cha,' she grinned. Grabbing a sparkling gold shawl, she announced, 'Welcome your *Strictly* stars Katie and Oliva, live on stage tonight! The crowd roars with applause.' Olivia smiled. 'Or imagine, Liv, we're nervously waiting backstage for our spot on *It Takes Two*. Zoe Ball calls dramatically, "Welcome the awesome Katie and Olivia!" The crowd go wild!'

'What, Zoe?' Katie shouted, a little louder, 'You love our cha-cha-cha?'

'You know what, Katie, it's funny how we can go from crying to laughing in minutes. Did your mum get you the book yet?' Liv asked.

'It should be here tomorrow,' said Katie.

'I don't care what Amber says – sticks and stones, and all that!'

'Let's do day 10 together of *You've Got the Power*!'

'OK.'

Then they both burst out laughing, singing, 'I've got the power, you've got the power, we've got the power …'

Paula thinks:

Olivia's fears around public performance and not being good enough or being rejected are intensified because she still has lots of grief inside, which she doesn't feel strong enough to look at. Of course, public performance is big on its own and the majority of kids and adults feel nervous around doing it.

Doing the magic 3 and flicking the confidence switch daily for a week will really help Olivia calm her emotions and build up her confidence around performing and being visible.

Understandably, Olivia is arguing with reality and doesn't want to accept the tragedy of her mum's death. She is worried about the future - not sure if she can be happy without her mum. She is also naturally compassionate and optimistic,

and underneath all the confusion she senses anything is possible.

Remember, we see the world as we are and not as it is. Olivia clearly doesn't have frizzy hair, but she is doubting herself because she's nervous about performing for the first time, letting Amber's words in and making herself upset. She is clearly comparing herself with others and deciding she's not enough.

As she starts to get to grips with changing her mindset from worry to wonder she will naturally become more empowered, and this will help her deal with her emotions and feel safe enough to talk about them and ask for help.

Katie is her cheerleading friend and mentor at this point, helping her face her worries and encouraging her to trust 'she's got the power'.

Day 10

Be Kind to Yourself

Sometimes we might feel we don't come up to scratch. We compare ourselves with our mates, with the good-looking one, with the brainy one, with the popular one, with the one with the big house and the rich parents. The truth is, nobody could ever be as good at being you as you are. It's all about accepting what is. Self-acceptance might sound soft, but it's actually very powerful. Our power is in choosing to be the very best and most awesome version of our amazing self that we can be – warts and all!

In Japan there is an ancient philosophy called wabi-sabi. It relates to the quirks and irregularities that come out of the process of making an object by hand. Take a ceramic handmade bowl, for instance – the bowl is considered to be more beautiful because of, not despite, its slight bumps, or cracks, or mistakes because those are what make it unique and fascinating.

Wabi-sabi nurtures all that is authentic by acknowledging three simple realities: nothing lasts, nothing is finished and nothing is perfect.

In less fancy terms, wabi-sabi is your favourite tattered old trainers, your favourite book or comic that's bent and battered with use, your favourite teddy with one eye, or your nana with her lined face. It's the painting you did which didn't turn out as you'd expected but you love it anyway. It is also you!

Trust me – I know the journey has had its ups and downs so far, but we are now entering a brave, new, special world where with *You've Got the Power* we're changing our approach, and the rewards are at hand. We shall soon be manifesting miracles and playing the game of life to the best of our potential, accepting every little bit of ourselves along the way.

You are unique. Look at it this way: nobody else has taken on this journey like you because nobody else has your memories. If you wrote a book about your adventure, good and bad, I promise you, there would be no other book like it. And I for one think that is something to celebrate. Cheers!

Acceptance really is the magic word to fire up our inner power! In these next exercises, I'm going to give you some super-effective tools for helping you accept and love yourself exactly as you are!

DAY 10: POWERFUL CHOICES FOR ME, MYSELF AND I

Do the magic 3. Now put on your thinking cap and have a go at the following.

Write down three ways you can accept yourself more, with examples, thinking about wabi-sabi:

1. _____

2. _____

3. _____

Three actions you can take to be more kind to yourself and to improve your confidence:

1. _____

2. _____

3. _____

Three negative thoughts you have about yourself that you're willing to ditch today:

1. _____

2. _____

3. _____

---

*Wanting to be someone else
is a waste of who you are.*

—Kurt Cobain

DAY TEN ☀ POWER POINTS TO REMEMBER

Did you know that everyone in the world has a completely unique fingerprint – no other person has the same finger print, even an identical twin! You are unique and there is only one of you, so don't try to be someone else because the job is taken. Be the best version of yourself that you can be in life. It's pointless comparing yourself with others and trying to be them: just be yourself. It is without doubt the best option, and it's what you were born to do!

Consider this statement and then finish the following sentence three times:

YOU ARE UNIQUE — OWN YOUR POWER

∞ EVERYONE IS UNIQUE AND FASCINATING. THERE IS NOT ONE OTHER PERSON ON THE PLANET THE SAME AS ME. I VALUE MYSELF AND MY UNIQUENESS. ∞

Three ways I can accept my uniqueness and harness my talents are:

1. _____

2. _____

3. _____

Day 10 affirmation

∞ I am unique and valuable. I breathe in inspiration; I breathe out the freedom to be me. ∞

😺 Superpower Song for day 10:

🎧 'True to Your Heart' by 98 Degrees and Stevie Wonder, ♪ from the movie *Mulan*

Day 11

The Happiness Effect

It goes without saying that happiness is something we all want to feel. That's only natural, and healthy too. But here's a thing: delirious happiness as a constant state is not realistic. This is a myth that we've been told so many times it feels like the truth. Nobody feels totally happy all the time – and if someone tells you they do, well, there are probably some little white lies going on. Like all emotional states, happiness is an experience in life. You're off the hook, because it's perfectly normal and human to not be happy all the time.

Acceptance of our experiences can make us feel more open and relaxed all the time, which makes our relationship with ourselves and others feel so much better. The good news is that **you do have the power** to increase the amount of good feelings you experience – in other words, you can up your happiness level! So, let's experience this idea a little more.

Remember when you last felt really happy, so happy you wanted to run and leap and hug your mates? Maybe you got good grades at school or had a really fun day with your best friends; maybe your team won a match or you got exactly what you wanted for your birthday. You wanted to hold on tight to that joyful feeling, so it would never leave you. But what happened? It's my guess some other feeling came along and took its place because stuff keeps happening that influences your mood.

We all go through a whole spectrum of feelings and emotional states; some we love, some we hate. Remember, you affect your feelings by how you think. You wouldn't go to your favourite patisserie and order a slice of hate with a squirt of jealousy on the side, so why keep feeding yourself hurtful thoughts? I know it's hard when we are hurt not to hang on to our pain, but you have the power to remember, 'This too shall pass,' breathe and remember the good stuff in your life too.

They say what we give we receive, so that's why I think it's brilliant to be gentle on yourself. Look, I know we also get sad, mad, anxious or hurt at times – and that's normal, we don't want to deny our feelings – but we can transform (take the sting out of) them by being our own best mate with a hug of acceptance, a sprinkle of kindness and a spotlight of awareness that it's just part of life, it doesn't define us and it will pass as soon as we let it!

DAY 11: WHAT MAKES YOU HAPPY?

There are lots of practical ways you can learn to create more happy vibes and positive thoughts in your everyday life. Imagination rules the world. Whether you think you can or you can't, you are right! Both you and I know this is true, even though we don't always want to believe it.

You can raise your happy vibes by tapping into the things that make your heart sing and make you feel connected. But you need to get to know what feeling happy feels like to you, before you can tap into it. When you follow your heart, you also follow your inspiration or intuition. Intuition just means the power to understand something without thinking it through in a logical way. It just feels right.

Maybe we write songs or poems naturally without being taught, or have a natural talent at art, music, sport or the sciences. Your intuition can point the way to what makes you happy and to a great thing to do in life. Steve Jobs of Apple said, '**Intuition is a very powerful thing, more powerful than intellect, in my opinion.**'

When you choose a more loving perspective it feels lovely and you are more connected to life and in touch with your intuition. Think about the ocean – it is just there, vast and abundant. When we feel sad and separate it's as though we are a little drop of water and we forget we are connected to the ocean. Fear makes us feel isolated and alone, whereas love unites and connects us. Sure, as an individual drop of water we can still feel happiness – we are just doing the best we can. However, getting the power means you know we are all connected, just like wave and ocean, and we have a bigger vision of life.

Remember, you are leaving the ordinary world and awakening to an extraordinary new world where your old beliefs are being questioned and you get powerful new insights. It's great because we question the rules and decide what life is about for you! I love that the Dalai Lama says, '**Learn the rules so you know how to break them properly.**' Having tuned into what makes you feel happy and in flow, you may even decide to change a few old 'I can't do's' to 'I can do.' That's cool – it just means you are braver than you thought. A little tip: when we are truly in flow and feeling happy it is as though time doesn't exist!

Practice: Guided visualisation

💜 Find a comfy, quiet place to sit or lie, close your eyes, and spend a moment bringing your attention to your breathing and letting your body settle.

💜 Let's become an imagination master and direct our thinking to all the times we felt good, happy or content. Think of a time when you last felt really happy.

♥ Spend just a few minutes really getting to know what this happiness feels like. Does it have a colour and texture? Where is it in your body? What things were making you happy?

♥ What was the event, where were you, what special people were there, or animals, or nature? What colours, what sounds, smells, places?

♥ Did you experience a sense of achievement or accomplishment, or other feelings such as confidence, intuition, inspiration or joy?

♥ Take five to ten minutes to let your mind wander and your imagination flow, then gently open your eyes when you're ready.

DAY ELEVEN ☀ POWER POINTS TO REMEMBER

Hey, at the end of the day we all want to happy; let's face it, who wants to be sad? The thing is, as we said earlier, we need to expand our story around happiness to include things like contentment, peace, freedom, joy, stillness and the like. That way we create realistic expectations, whilst also remembering sometimes we'll feel, sad, lonely, cross, annoyed or bored, and it's important not to label all

HAPPINESS IS A JOURNEY, NOT A DESTINATION

of those feelings as stress. We have a brilliant range of emotions and it's cool to own them all.

Consider this statement and then finish the following sentence three times:

∞ I LOVE ALL THE DIFFERENT EMOTIONS IN LIFE. I LOVE MY SENSES AND I EXPERIENCE LIFE JUST AS IT COMES, WITHOUT EXPECTATION. I LET GO OF THE NEED TO CONTROL. ∞

Three unrealistic ways I think I have to be happy all the time are:

1. _____

2. _____

3. _____

Day 11 affirmation

∞ I can increase my happiness; I am unique and amazing;
I am a miracle. I breathe in relaxation; I breathe out happiness. ∞

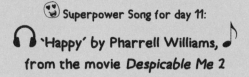 Superpower Song for day 11:
🎧 'Happy' by Pharrell Williams, ♪
from the movie *Despicable Me 2*

Day 12

Powerful Choices for Me, Myself and I

Do the magic 3. Make a list of things that make you happy below. Don't think about it too hard, just list things that come to mind, such as 'my cat', 'roast dinners', 'cycle rides', 'laughing with my best friends', 'football after school', 'Netflix on the sofa'.

1. _____

2. _____

3. _____

4. _____

5. _____

6. _____

Make a list of happy memories from the most recent ones to further back. Take a look to work out if these memories have anything in common – maybe you felt free or more alive in all of them. Is there a theme?

1. _____

2. _____

3. _____

4. _____

5. _____

6. _____

Think of three things you could do to make yourself feel happier in day-to-day life. Why not commit to taking action to do these things, starting now?

1. _____

2. _____

3. _____

For every minute you are angry
you lose sixty seconds of happiness.

DAY 12: FLICK THE HAPPINESS SWITCH

Power exercise: 10 minutes

Remember a time when you felt really happy, or imagine one that will make you happy.

Now imagine this happy memory/thought as a movie screen and you are in the movie – see yourself larger than life right there on the screen. Using your imagination, continue to visualise what you saw, heard and felt, and really connect with how good it was. Who is there? Are you laughing? Where are you? What are the sounds and smells?

See the screen of 'your life' really bright with vivid colours. What can you hear? As you think about the memory, turn up the sound and the brightness on your screen.

To help you remember this really happy time you can create a little reminder. Try squeezing your thumb and first finger together on your right hand as you think about your happy memory. This squeezing action can become a new trigger to bring back your happy memory. A bit like a magic power button – or a happiness switch.

This way, next time you are feeling bad, lonely or sad, just squeeze your thumb and first finger and remember your happy memory. This is your happy switch and you can use it whenever you need to relax or feel better.

When you are in a tricky situation, take a breath and 'view' it. This can help you see more clearly what's going on. Imagine you are watching a play and you are one of the actors – it might help you see what's going on for the other characters too. Check out the type of role you are playing. Are you happy with how you are behaving? Maybe without the stress you would behave a bit more kindly?

DAY TWELVE ☀ POWER POINTS TO REMEMBER

It turns out, and the research proves it, that when we watch happy movies, remember happy times or read happy stories we feel happy. This also means when we watch scary/stressful movies, remember stressful times, or read or gossip about stressful things we can feel more stressed. Remember, the brain can't tell the difference between what is real and imagined, so all experiences are strengthening neuropathways. Just as happiness is good for your health, it makes sense that the opposite, stress, erodes your well-being.

Consider this statement and then finish the following sentence three times.

∞ MY WELL-BEING IS IMPORTANT TO ME. EVERY ACTION I TAKE
IS ADDING TO MY WELL-BEING OR TAKING AWAY FROM IT.
I AM THE CREATOR AND I CAN CREATE MIRACLES. ∞

Little miracles I can create to be kind in my thoughts to myself and others are:

1. _____

2. _____

3. _____

MY THOUGHTS AND DREAMS CAN CREATE
MIRACLES — I CREATE WITH MY THOUGHTS

Day 12 affirmation

∞ Today I choose not to judge myself or others.
I breathe in love; I breathe out miracles. ∞

😊 Superpower Song for day 12:

🎧 'Breaking Free' by Troy and Gabriella Montez, ♪
from the movie *High School Musical*

Day 13

Creating a 'Dream Board'

The creative brain is also the one that helps us fulfil our dreams, so get crafty with a **dream board**. A dream board is simply a display of images, photographs, keepsakes and words that helps you to record and celebrate good times. You could do it in a scrapbook or as part of your journal – it doesn't have to be a dream *board*, but it is fun making one.

What you'll need:

⭐ A large piece of cardboard – I like to use cork/net memo boards or artists' canvas to pin things on; this way we can change the board as our dreams change.

⭐ Old magazines, Internet pictures, pamphlets, etc.

⭐ Glue or other adhesive, colourful pens, glitter (of course!)

⭐ Any other fun things that float your boat!

What to do:

⭐ Go through the magazines and cut out any pictures that motivate you, and current dreams; make sure what you choose feels great (content) and ambitious.

⭐ You can also divide the board into four sections. Here are some ideas for what to include:

● **Do:** What do you want to do in the next six months? What do you enjoy doing? What would you like to learn to do?

● **Be:** What do you want to be when you grow up? What kind of person do you want to be? (Find photos of smiling faces, hearts, people helping others, success, etc.)

● **Go:** Where do you dream of going? Where have you already been? What's your favourite place to visit? How will you get there?

● **Love:** Who do you love? Family? Pets? What makes you feel loved?

Avoid filling in your board with toys and material possessions. Place your dream board in your bedroom, where it can remind you of how amazing your life can be.

DAY 13: JOY BREATHING

Over the next few days, find just five or ten minutes each day to exercise your happiness muscles. This will make them stronger and create more happy vibes in your life. Try the exercise below. It's not hard to do, and it will make you feel fantastic! **Remember, you can use the exercise here alongside all the other happiness and power exercises in this book.**

⭐ Find somewhere where you can sit quietly for a few minutes. Become aware of your body and your posture, and gently focus on your breath going in and out. Once you feel settled, remember a time you felt really joyful, then simply breathe into those feelings of happiness. Try to really put yourself right back into the time you are thinking about, then turn up the brightness on the image you have. Try to magnify any sensations of joy you are feeling in your physical body, or listen for the joy and laughter you may be hearing and turn up the volume.

⭐ Now bring your attention back to your breath and gently draw the breath into your heart. Imagine it is warm, like golden rays of glorious sunshine, and on the out-breath let that light flood your whole being with warm, cosy, secure, happy feelings.

⭐ Your heart becomes like a mini-sun within your chest, shining a flood of warmth and happiness throughout your body with every out-breath.

Dreaming fuels our passion for life and it's exciting to daydream and wonder about all the amazing things you can do in life. It's wonderful to make plans and inspire yourself to keep your achievements on track, and celebrate the things you love. It really helps you get focused and happy about life.

Consider this statement and then finish the following sentence three times.

FOLLOW YOUR DREAMS - THEY POINT IN
THE DIRECTION OF YOUR GREATNESS

∞ I LOVE IMAGINING MY FUTURE. DREAMING MAKES ME FEEL
GOOD AND CREATES POSITIVE ENERGY IN MY LIFE.
MY DREAMS BECOME REALITY; HOW EXCITING,
I CAN CREATE A WONDERFUL LIFE. ∞

Three ways I like to dream up my future are:

1. _____

2. _____

3. _____

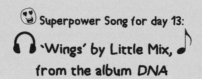

Day 13 affirmation

∞ I love dreaming – it feels great. I breathe in optimism; I breathe out joy. ∞

🎧 Superpower Song for day 13:
🎧 'Wings' by Little Mix, ♪
from the album DNA

Day 14

Recap on Worry and Wonder

Let's have a little review of the wonder-and-worry mindset.
The mind likes what's familiar and that's why we can often resist change. That means the shoulda, woulda, coulda doubts can attack like missiles, and we'll need to get bulletproof if we are to only let in the wonder mindset.

INSTEAD OF:	TRY:
Fighting with Reality	① Accepting 'what is'
I am not enough	② Embracing your Uniqueness
I can't Ask for help	③ Being Grateful
Worrying about the past	④ Knowing what you want
I need to control the future	⑤ Anything is possible
Running on FEAR:	⑥ Being mindful and compassionate
False Evidence Appearing Real	
I'm not as good as them	⑦ Seeing we are all connected

How are you doing moving from the seven worries to the seven wonders of thinking? Getting your head around changing your thinking is pivotal to your success, that's why I am giving you another look at the above picture. Let's take it one step further. Why not copy it out and place it in prominent places around your house like your bedroom mirror, the bathroom mirror or your fridge. Place it on the inside of your school books, so that when you open them you are reminded again. Learning a new mindset is like learning a new language; we need constant reminders to get a handle on it.

Remember – we think around 60 to 80,000 thoughts a day, so best to try to make them support us! It's also a fact that it takes more muscles to frown than to smile, so turn that frown upside down and save your precious power!

DAY 14: SQUEEZE THAT STRESS OUT

Let's relax. Did you know relaxing helps you get the power mindset? When we are relaxed our bodies feel calm and peaceful and we are often kinder to ourselves as a result.

Power practice: This is a quick progressive muscle relaxation that will allow you to focus on key areas where stress can build up in your body.

⭐ Tense and relax each area I mention. When you tense the area, do not cause any pain. Tighten only until you feel tension. If you feel any discomfort, stop or ease up.

⭐ Work through the body tensing and relaxing the muscles, and do a couple of examples exaggerating the movements.

⭐ Screw up your face like a raisin for a count of three. It's okay if it makes you laugh at first, that can even help as it reduces tension. Do this a couple of times. Then move through the body, following the process: tighten, hold, feel and release.

⭐ Raise your shoulders up towards your ears ... tighten the muscles there ... hold ... feel the tension there ... and now release. Let your shoulders drop to a lower, more comfortable position. Now move through the rest of the body.

DAY FOURTEEN ☀ POWER POINTS TO REMEMBER

As we said earlier, our thinking is literally creating our life, and we can let either fear or fun fuel our life. The thing is that all the stress in the world is not going to change events that have already happened, and stressing over what might happen is just creating a reality that doesn't help anyone, least of all you. Wonder feels lighter and it looks lighter. Fear is really busy, and that's what it does to our mind – it makes it race, resending painful accusations of the hero, you, not being good enough! Time to direct a feel-good, bestseller life!

Consider this statement and then finish the following sentence three times:

I DON'T LABEL SITUATIONS –
I AM OPEN TO FRESH STARTS

∞ I LET WORRY GO – IT DOESN'T HELP ME. I
AM THE CREATOR OF MY LIFE; I CHOOSE WONDER. WONDER
IS LIKE A BEGINNER MIND, AS THOUGH WE ARE SEEING
LIFE FOR THE FIRST TIME – E.G., WITH NO JUDGEMENT – SO
MAYBE WE CAN FORGIVE OR GIVE IT A GO. ∞

Three ways I can bring wonder into my life and create a beginner mind are:

1. _____

2. _____

3. _____

Day 14 affirmation

∞ I look at life with wonder. I breathe in safety; I breathe out adventure. ∞

😊 Superpower Song for day 14:

🎧 'Shine' by Take That, ♪
from the album *Beautiful World*

😊 Week 1 inspiration:

'Jim Carrey: From the Factory to the Funhouse',
published on YouTube by Street Fighter – https://youtu.be/JhbZD2_bHhw

WEEK THREE

THE AMAZING WORLD OF YOU

ACT TWO – INITIATION

- ✔ Crossing the first threshold
- ✔ Tests, allies, enemies

---

*A winner is a dreamer
who never gives up.*

—Nelson Mandela

ACT TWO – INITIATION

Crossing the first threshold: For you, my gorgeous hero, life will never be the same: you are done with ordinary world, the old way of being is over. A mini-miracle has occurred in your life – you've changed your perception and there is no going back. This is where the adventure of self-discovery truly begins and we are about to dive deep into the unknown, so get ready, our journey to the special world begins. This is the point of no return, you're trusting in the knowledge **you've got the power**, and this means you're ready to ditch worry and switch on wonder in your mindset.

Tests, allies, enemies: I know it's tricky – you're learning the rules of your new world, and challenges and conflicts will arise. You're smashing your boundaries, which is great, making new friends and having new experiences, yet at the same time more tests are coming your way. During this time, you'll need to rock your resilience; it will test your strength of will as you come face to face with foes or demon thoughts. This stage is all about preparing you to rise to your goal or challenge and take your consciousness on a new adventure.

Approach to your innermost cave: This stage is tough – you have to be with your fear. It may be actual physical fears, or an inner conflict that you're struggling with that you haven't faced yet. It's your metaphorical dragon (fire-breathing thoughts of doom and gloom) that guards your treasure and holds you back. It isn't easy and it feels scary as you have to make the tough decision **to feel the fear and do it anyway** if you are to retrieve the biggest rewards. By going deep within yourself you'll find the courage to conquer the dragon (fear thoughts) and gain the brilliant rewards (treasure) of more confidence and happiness.

Ordeal: This stage can feel like a life-or-death crisis. You'll experience overcoming a major hurdle or obstacle (the challenge or goal you want to achieve that frightens you). This is usually the biggest ordeal and you basically die (metaphorically) to the old way of being (thinking), and from this you experience a resurrection which gives you more power and insight in order to fulfil your destiny. You've got this. Connected to your inner power you'll purify your fear thinking and sacrifice all the ways you've been compromising your happiness. It's another moment of death and rebirth and ascension in your thinking. You have used your inner power to create higher-vibe thinking by overcoming the worries of the world that created your conflict at the beginning of your adventure.

Day 15

Leaving the Worry World Behind

OK, we are at the true turning point. Phew! The most important part of leaving the worry world behind is **the choice to be kind to ourselves**. Being kind to yourself involves consistent self-care and compassion, which means being loving, understanding and patient with yourself. We know kindness makes us happier and it's great for our well-being. I mean, check out what the greatest scientific minds across the planet have proved about how stress and kindness affect our mood:

What stress does to the body	What kindness does to the body
Creates low-mood chemicals	Creates feel-good chemicals
Can make us anxious and irritable	Makes us optimistic
Can make us unhappy	Makes us happy
Creates tension and wobbles	Relaxes our nervous system
Clouds the mind – fuzzy thinking	Brings clarity and focus – great for exams
Decreases creativity	Enhances creativity
Suppresses the immune system	Boosts the immune system
Can make you isolate yourself	Helps you make friends and connect
May trigger unhappiness	Often triggers joy

Power thoughts: Can you think of how love and kindness have helped you when you have felt sad, small, alone, afraid or even angry? Feeling happy comes in many forms – it might have been a kind text or Instagram message from a friend, a hug from your mum or dad, a kind word from a teacher, or a mate helping you with tricky homework.

It's powerful to think kind thoughts about yourself. By now we are all over the fact that **what you think about comes about**, so your thinking is a major superpower, and we can charge that and your happy vibes up using affirmations. An affirmation is just a statement that makes you feel good, that you can say to yourself, either out loud or in your head – you can even write it on a piece of paper and put it on your mirror, the fridge, your books or anywhere, really, as a reminder. You can use the affirmations at the end of each day in this book to boost your wonder power.

Repeating affirmations helps your brain to make strong neuropathways that will make being kind to yourself with your internal chatter easier. Each time you think a thought, you are creating a well-trodden path to either wonder or worry. Think of a field where people create a path in the grass because they keep walking along the same route – that's what happens in your brain too: we create neuropathways in the field of our brain by how we think. If we think anything enough it becomes a belief, where the path is so well worn we walk down it without questioning it – we have created a habit.

Affirmations help us unlearn beliefs and release unhealthy habits. They have to feel right for you, though – it's easier if we **believe it to achieve it**! How will I know? Easy! Say, 'I am – your name –': notice that feels right and true. Yes? OK, now say, 'I am Justin Bieber' or 'I am Ariana Grande' – notice that feels weird and daft. Yes? That's how you know your affirmation is right for you – it feels right. You could play Pharrell Williams's 'Happy' song – you can't help but smile – when you write yours. Here are a few examples so you get the vibe:

'Every day in every way I am getting happier!'

'I love happy feelings and I can feel them every day.'

'Happiness is easy because I deserve to be happy.'

'I am inspired – things get easier for me daily.'

'I am a queen/king happy-hormone maker.'

'I am happy and free.'

'I am doing my best – I am enough.'

Remember, constantly worrying about things is just making affirmations that make you feel bad.

DAY FIFTEEN ☀ POWER POINTS TO REMEMBER

Mindfulness is about paying attention here and now with kindness and curiosity, and that means paying attention to our thoughts, speech and actions. Are you being kind to yourself? Do you talk kindly to yourself and treat yourself well? Would you say to your best friend the type of things you say to yourself in your mind?

Consider this statement and then finish the following sentence three times:

WHEN I AM KIND TO MYSELF,
EVERYONE BENEFITS

∞ I STOP CRITICISING MYSELF - IT DOESN'T HELP ME. I AM THE CREATOR OF MY LIFE, AND I CHOOSE TO BE KIND TO MYSELF. I CAN ONLY BE AS KIND TO ANOTHER AS I AM TO MYSELF; THEREFORE, BEING KIND TO ME IS BETTER FOR EVERYONE. ∞

Three areas where I can bring more self-care and compassion to myself are:

1. _____

2. _____

3. _____

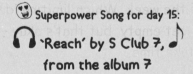

Day 15 affirmation

∞ I take care of myself. I breathe in compassion;
I breathe out self-love. ∞

🎧 Superpower Song for day 15:
🎧 'Reach' by S Club 7, ♪
from the album 7

Day 16

Power Chill – Relaxation Is Power!

No one can just make themselves calm overnight these days. What with school, homework, clubs – and that's before we get to friends and family – we're so busy! 'Hang on,' you might think, 'is there time for relaxation?' Of course – we make it; we are in control. I know, with all this pressure it's a miracle we are not even more stressed, but, listen, we can change that. Let's bring on the **power mindset**, for today your mission, if you choose to accept it, is to lay low like lettuce. You know what I mean – just be still.

It turns out that when we get quiet and calmer inside we feel less stressed and more creative. Back to the lettuce – let's get curious and just watch others and how they respond with either the wonder or the worry mindset. You could even ask your friends and family five things they do to feel more still. Write in your journal five things that make you feel more relaxed.

As the week goes on, keep a note in your journal of the strategies you notice that help people stay relaxed under pressure. Which ones could you do? Remember, challenge your old thinking, and check out the 'is-it-true? jar' at the end of the week. Which limiting ideas would you let go of now? The jar might not get empty, but that's okay – we are rewiring our thoughts and that can take time.

Power thinking: Imagine a peaceful world – how would that be? What does it look like? How would it feel? Explore your vision for the world. As a final mission of the week, ask yourself, 'What can I do to be more calm and kinder?' (qualities of the power mindset) in the following areas:

1. To myself: _____

2. In relationships: _____

3. To the world: _____

Remember, the truth is we all need to take action to have the confidence to live a great life. We all know Gandhi said, '**Be the change you want to see in the world.**' But did you know he also said, '**I'm so busy today, I will have to meditate twice as long!**'?

Look at what Gandhi achieved – it makes sense to show kindness and try to be calm, and it definitely takes courage.

DAY SIXTEEN ☀ POWER POINTS TO REMEMBER

Being mindful helps us see clearly where we are creating lions or love in our life. You know that every thought you think creates a physical reaction and an emotional response within you. When you feel bad, you are ruminating or resending thoughts of worry and pain to your body, and that hurts. Again, if you wouldn't say it to your best friend, don't say it to yourself.

I HAVE SELF-COMPASSION AND
I CHOOSE LOVE OVER FEAR

Consider this statement and then finish the following sentence three times.

∞ I CHOOSE LOVE OVER LIONS. I AM THE CREATOR OF MY LIFE AND I CHOOSE TO BE KIND TO MYSELF. I CAN GENERATE FEELINGS OF COURAGE BY HOW I THINK, ACT AND SPEAK. ∞

Three areas where I could turn fear thinking and feeling into excitement are:

1. _____

2. _____

3. _____

Day 16 affirmation

∞ I take care of myself. I breathe in compassion;
I breathe out self-love. ∞

😊 Superpower Song for day 16:

🎧 'When You Believe' by Michelle Pfeiffer and Sally Dworsky, ♪
from the movie *Prince of Egypt*

ACT TWO, WEEK THREE, FOR HARRY

Harry hated running and wished he'd never gotten himself into this, but at least Tom had agreed to come along for the ride.

He looked across the field in disbelief. Snake was talking to the coach. 'No. No. No.' boomed in his head.

'Please tell me he's not in the running club, shall we bin it?' He stared at Tom and then he stared some more. 'I feel sick,' he said, his belly doing somersaults.

Tom tried to encourage him: 'Come on, mate, he can't touch you on the track, in front of old Jonesy. It'll be alright.'

Harry's Jedi force was elusive as worry literally teleported through his body, and his legs felt weak. He could almost hear Vader (Snake): 'You dare to invade my space? My demands are non-negotiable. Do what I want, whenever I want it, or die!' red menace oozing from his eyes.

Harry felt like he would give anything to not be there. Cutting across his thoughts he heard, 'Harry, are you deaf, lad?' It was Mr Jones, jolting Harry back to the present moment.

'Sorry Sir, just, erm ...,' he stuttered incoherently.

'What? Never mind. Get on the start line with the beginners. Now, Harry, we haven't got all day,' demanded Mr Jones impatiently.

'Marks. Get set. Go.' Harry shot off the line like a bullet, to the surprise of the coach and the faster runners, including Snake. They watched on as Harry whizzed around the field, leaving the competition in his dust. He was brilliant. He crossed the finish line to cheers and loads of clapping.

'Who knew? Great run, Harry. Well done,' beamed Mr Jones. 'Speed like that will get you on the first squad.'

'No way,' thought Harry. 'Am I actually good at this? Must be all the practice running from Snake and his puppets, or did I mean muppets? It's about time I told him to lay off me – I've had enough of him.' For the first time since arriving at the field Harry felt good.

'That was epic, mate,' shouted Tom as he came in about fifth across the line.

Mr Jones was clapping him on the back. 'Great. Great run, Harry. Brilliant!' he said.

Harry was grinning like a Cheshire cat, even smiling to himself, 'I have got the power!' Then chuckling, thinking his mum would be made up when he told her.

Even sardonic, sneering Snake couldn't ruin this moment. Or so he thought ...

FINISH LINE

Paula thinks:

Harry crosses the threshold from worry to wonder with his mindset. He's decided he has a choice – he doesn't have to put up with being bullied. He's beginning to embrace his uniqueness and truly accept he has the power.

Embracing kindness (promotes the relaxation response) instead of lions (promotes the stress response) in his thinking is also helping him feel less hypervigilant around Snake.

This is the change in perception that can transform his life, and there is no going back. He's making new connections and stretching his comfort zone. He is deciding he's enough and not comparing himself with others.

He now believes he can come face to face with his 'demon' Snake, as he's changing his thinking around his self-worth and building his courage, resilience and confidence. Adopting all of the practices given here over the last few weeks and turning on his endorphin flow regularly will not only be increasing his resilience, but also increasing his overall sense of well-being.

He is taking on board the power mindset of wonder and enjoying the fact he can change and improve his life by how he thinks, acts and speaks.

Remember, we have to believe it to achieve it!

ACT TWO, WEEK THREE, FOR OUR HERO OLIVIA

Pops was playing swing music in the background when Olivia arrived home. As soon as he saw her he chorused, '**Da**, **da**, **da**, **da**, **da**, **da**, daaaaa ...' as he gave her a hug.

She smiled. 'I don't know, Pops, all the fake tan, leotards and loads of make-up make me feel weird. I wish mum was still here ...'

Pops held her closer. 'Course you do, darling. I do too, Livy.'

'It's just she could help me with the costume. What if I look revolting? Do you think I'm fat, Pops? Is my hair too frizzy? I go so red and sweaty when I dance, I don't feel pretty.'

'You're beautiful and slender, Livy. Why would you think that?' asked Pops, bewildered.

'I just ... I am ... I don't ...' Confused, she couldn't form her sentence. Livy felt her heart beating and her hands shaking.'

'It's okay, love,' said Pops.

'Pops, they think we are so good, they want us to open the show with a solo. It's awful – how will I cope? You know I get nervous on stage, and everyone will be looking at me. What if I make a mistake?'

'It's normal to get nervous, Livy. We all do. It just means you care. You want to do well,' encouraged Pops. 'We can find a way to make that adrenaline work for you, so you perform even better. We still have a few weeks until the live show.'

Livy wasn't convinced. Then she felt calmer and knew her thinking was making her feel bad. '**You're right, Pops. I love dancing so much, I Can Do This. Why not? Goodbye worry. Hello wonder!**' She announced assertively, thinking, 'And it's been scientifically proven.'

DING, the doorbell rang.

'I'll get it, love.'

DING again.

'Hang on, I'm coming!' he shouted.

He opened the door. It was Katie.

'Where is she? I can't believe it – mum's got us backstage passes to *Strictly*!' she shrieked.

Katie burst through the lounge door. 'Did you hear that, Livy? We're going backstage on *Strictly*. Because that's just what **we do**, **darling**,' she *said*, with a triumphant smile flickering across her face. 'FAB-U-LOUS darling. FAB-U-LOUS ...' She grinned.

Paula thinks:

Yay for Olivia! There is no turning back – she has changed her mind and decided she's going to give the power mindset a go. Her demons aren't dragons to slay but thoughts and worries and comparing herself, worrying she's not good enough. She knows her worries diminish her well-being and make her feel bad.

All of the practices over the last few weeks will be helping Olivia feel more resilient and confident. She understands the mind/body connection and knows thoughts elicit feelings. It makes sense to be kind to herself and she has all the science to prove it, which appeals to her personality.

She's recognising that what we believe becomes reality and she wants to overcome her fears and do what she loves. She has crossed the first threshold and faced her enemy – worry thinking – and is beginning to accept she has the power to do what she wants.

She naturally wants to be optimistic, so rewiring her brain and changing her thinking will come naturally to her. She likes that she can trace the results to scientific research, making the experiment of changing the way she thinks a great choice in her mind. It still feels tricky, but at least now she is prepared to believe she can do it. Pops is her number-one supporter, although Katie is hot on his heels!

Day 17

Work Your Uniqueness!

Breathe ... Pay attention right here and right now with love, kindness and curiosity. Ignore those pings from your phone – although I thought we'd agreed to put it on silent. Didn't we?

Start to have a look at who you are: what's unique about you? Using your *You've Got the Power* journal, list all the things you think about yourself.

⭐ Include your roles – e.g., things like brother, sister, daughter, friend, student, leader, helper, carer, babysitter.

⭐ Include skills – e.g., good tennis player, brilliant at maths, a wonderful artist, good sense of humour, musical, organised, halo-like kind and caring, great dancer, amazing debater, genius, and darn-right awesome.

SMART Tip

Sometimes our mind runs on automatic pilot, which means just doing something without thinking about it or without making any effort, which is fine if we are not being mindless, but generally we are. The practice of mindfulness and meditation helps us to experience the present moment.

Mindfulness helps us connect to our health and well-being. We can see, talk, walk, laugh, jump, hug, write, read and a million other things, but without mindfulness we forget this. We even forget it's amazing we are alive and have the opportunity to do loads with our life! The human body is definitely the best creation on the planet, but we are so busy on our phones and other tech stuff we've forgotten that our organism beats any computer on the planet. Totally awesome.

SMART Tip

Write at least ten great things you think about yourself and ten mean things you think about yourself. Also list ten roles you have in life.

I know I keep banging on about mindfulness, but it's such a big deal in creating a powerful mindset. It really helps you get to grips with the rules of the mind. You know your mind always does what it thinks you want it to do, and mindfulness helps us experience the present moment, which means we will know when we are being our best friend or our worst enemy with our thinking.

Consider this statement and then finish the sentence below three times.

WE ARE WHAT WE THINK. ALL THAT WE ARE ARISES WITH OUR THOUGHTS. WITH OUR THOUGHTS, WE MAKE THE WORLD.

∞ BEING IN THE PRESENT MOMENT HELPS ME CREATE A POWERFUL NEW LIFE. I CAN NOTICE DESTRUCTIVE THOUGHTS AND CHOOSE TO CREATE A GROWTH MINDSET WITH MORE SELF-COMPASSION AND KINDNESS. ∞

Three ways I can be more mindful and treat myself better are:

1. _____

2. _____

3. _____

Mindfulness helps me see clearly
how I create my mindset

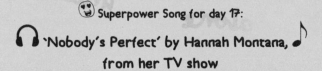

Day 17 affirmation

∞ I love being mindful, it helps me create a powerful life. I breathe in awareness; I breathe out love and kindness. ∞

😊 Superpower Song for day 17:

🎧 'Nobody's Perfect' by Hannah Montana, 🎵
from her TV show

Day 18

Getting to Know You!

Draw two stick people. Now write your worries around one and your wonder around the other. There are examples below.

'When my thoughts worry me and I think I can't – or I can't accept myself – I think/feel/act in ways which make me experience:'

Hey, I feel you. You know what you think about is felt in your body, and you know you're in charge of your thinking – so, a big responsibility, hey? You know there are pleasant, unpleasant and neutral sensations, and you can accept that if you keep resending painful thoughts through your body it's like ordering a pizza with painful toppings.

You've got the power to choose to care for yourself and explore your wonder mindset, whilst accepting painful stuff happens, just like happy stuff happens too.

Enough of that – tell me about the wonder mindset!

'When I feel wonder with my thoughts and I think I can – and I accept myself and know I am enough – I remember my talents and I think/feel/act in ways which make me experience:'

Once you've done your two versions of thinking you really get to notice how thoughts do affect your feelings, and of course feelings affect actions, like we could laugh or cry. Building your wonder mindset is an inside job – remember, you are rewiring your brain for more love and kindness or confidence and calm in your life, one thought at a time. And – you've got it – the greatest minds across the planet have come together on thousands of occasions with study after study to prove this is true. Heroes don't compare their journey to someone else's. Where you are and where you're headed are completely unique to you. Focus only on your next small step.

DAY EIGHTEEN ☀ POWER POINTS TO REMEMBER

Remember, mindfulness is about paying attention to the here and now, with kindness and curiosity, and to the sensations that we feel. When we are aware of sensations as they arise within our body, we become more connected to our sense of well-being. This kind of deep listening to ourselves really helps us learn how to self-regulate our responses and have kindness and patience towards ourselves.

Consider this statement and then finish the following sentence three times.

∞ BEING IN TOUCH WITH MY BODY AND EMOTIONS AND SENSATIONS HELPS ME MANAGE MY MIND, BODY, EMOTIONS AND SPIRIT. BEING PRESENT HERE AND NOW HELPS ME CARE FOR MYSELF AND CONNECT TO MY INNER SPIRIT OF POWER. ∞

Three ways I can show myself I am listening to my feelings and taking care of my physical body now are:

1. _____

2. _____

3. _____

WHEN I AM KIND TO MYSELF, EVERYONE BENEFITS.

Day 18 affirmation

∞ I take care of myself and deepen my breathing; I listen to my body. I breathe in presence; I breathe out empathy. ∞

🐾 Superpower Song for day 18:

🎧 'Brave' by Sara Bareilles, ♪
from the album *The Blessed Unrest*

Day 19

Creating Powerful Thoughts for Me, Myself and I

Do the magic 3, then put on your thinking cap. What negative things do you tell yourself about yourself? This might also include not feeling good enough and comparisons to others. For example:

'I'm not pretty enough'; 'I should be thinner, stronger, taller'; 'I'm bad at sport'; 'I'm lazy';' 'I'm stupid'; I'm rubbish at drawing, or maths, or French'; 'There's something wrong with me – people don't like me.'

Write down four of your own examples:

1. _____

2. _____

3. _____

4. _____

Once you've listed them, really think about whether they are true. If you were a detective, what would your evidence be? Can you find evidence to counteract this thought? For example, you might say to yourself: 'I'm really bad at sport – I just can't do it.' Is this entirely true?

You might not be good at football or netball, but perhaps you love to swim, or do cartwheels, or play on the bars in the park. Perhaps you might think you're rubbish at English or art, but you're great at creating funny Instagram posts, or baking and icing a beautiful cake? List some more:

1. _____

2. _____

3. _____

4. _____

It might feel a bit difficult, especially if you are really honest, but don't worry, this is the first step to turning your negatives into positives.

It is important to accept our thinking and not deny how we think or feel; however, it is equally important to remember **thoughts are not facts** and we can decide what we think, say and do.

It's my wonderful life power-mindset thinking

If it feels overwhelming, chat to a parent or friend about how your thinking is making you feel awful – calling yourself an idiot or not good enough is never going to teleport happiness or resilience around your body.

The fact is you'd never say to your best mate, 'You're an idiot,' 'No one likes you,' 'Of course you can't do it – why would you bother?' Would you? No, you would not and you'd probably have no friends if you did! So, it stops here. Stop speaking to yourself like that silently in your head. It's time to be your own best friend and the hero of your lovely intuitive heart.

Power-mindset thinking tips

💜 I am growing, I am getting better. I know how powerful my mind is and I know I can speak great feelings into my life.

💜 I can change my life. Change starts with me. If I am not happy, I can change the way I think and the action I take.

💜 I know I am not my past, and I stop worrying about the future.

💜 I am great. I am not my mistakes or mis-takes in the movie of my life.

💜 No problem or challenge can take away my power to choose to support myself. I know what I focus on I feel, and I know happiness, peace and joy are an inside job.

💜 I choose to know that I will make it. I feed my self-esteem and resilience.

Connect to the hero in your heart – believe in yourself.

DAY NINETEEN ☀ POWER POINTS TO REMEMBER

We know the mind learns by repetition and that practice makes perfect. I know you can't believe I am going to remind you again, but I have to – it is a big deal. You are creating your world with every thought you have. Your inner world reflects what you see on the outside. If you feel self-confidence it's infectious – other people feel it too. If you feel lacking in self-esteem others feel that too, and may think they can take advantage of you as a result.

Consider this statement and then finish the following sentence three times.

I CREATE A WONDERFUL LIFE WITH MY AMAZING, BRILLIANT THINKING.

∞ I EXPECT THE BEST - I KNOW MY VALUE AND SELF-WORTH. THE MORE I TREAT MYSELF WELL THE BETTER OTHERS TREAT ME. MY EXTERNAL WORLD IS THE OUTER EXPRESSION OF MY INNER WORLD OF THOUGHTS AND FEELINGS. ∞

Three thoughts I can have to increase my happiness and confidence are:

1. _____

2. _____

3. _____

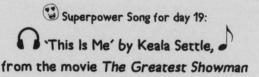

Day 19 affirmation

∞ I choose to notice how brilliant, confident, kind and lovely I am. I breathe in confidence; I breathe out self-love. ∞

😜 Superpower Song for day 19:
🎧 'This Is Me' by Keala Settle, ♪
from the movie *The Greatest Showman*

Day 20

The Garden of My Life

Inquiry: What does your garden grow?

I think it's helpful to think of your mind as a garden. You can choose what you have growing in there. You can sow the seeds and you can water and feed them. Weeds will always try to worm their way through, but if you're tending your garden and keeping a regular eye on it – in other words, regular practice of mindfulness and meditation – you can keep the weeds at bay.

Cut back those ugly weeds (thoughts/words/actions):

If you could change/improve six things/behaviours about yourself, what would they be?

1. _____   4. _____

2. _____   5. _____

3. _____   6. _____

Sow more good seeds (thoughts/words/actions):

If you had six golden seeds, what would you plant in your life?

1. _____   4. _____

2. _____   5. _____

3. _____   6. _____

When you feel like giving up, remember why you started. Remind yourself of the positive change you want to create. You've got the power and your future is bright.

DAY 20: RELAX, JUST DO IT – BEAUTIFUL RAINBOW OF LIGHT

Find a comfortable, quiet place to sit. Close your eyes and focus on the in and out of your breath until you feel settled and calm.

Imagine a beautiful, coloured rainbow floating above your head. See all the colours – the pinks and the blues, the greens and the yellows, the oranges and the reds, maybe there is also some gold and silver. Take a few moments to really notice what colours your beautiful rainbow is.

As you breathe, this awesome rainbow grows larger and larger and comes closer and closer and starts to gently wash over you. As it does, your whole being relaxes and all the colours fill your body. You go inside and find that special calm place where you feel totally relaxed and peaceful.

As you breathe, you are totally safe in the rainbow light. Totally safe. Totally protected and very, very comfortable.

DAY TWENTY ☀ POWER POINTS TO REMEMBER

So, how does your garden grow? With silver bells and cockle shells? ... Is it overgrown with weeds (unhelpful thinking) or is it a creation to behold of magical miracles you want in your life? Maybe it's a bit of mix? Whatever it looks like, you have the ability to change it by adopting your power mindset and being the gardener of your world.

I AM THE CREATOR OF MY DESTINY: I BELIEVE IN MYSELF.

Consider this statement and then finish the following sentence three times.

∞ I GROW MY LIFE WITH MAGIC AND MIRACLES.
I KNOW MY MIND RESPONDS TO THE PICTURES AND WORDS
I PROGRAM IT WITH, AS THOUGH THEY WERE ALREADY REAL.
I CAN FAKE IT TILL I MAKE IT, AND ONLY SEE THE BEST
GARDEN ON THE PLANET FOR ME. ∞

Three ways I can visualise a brilliant, cool and confident life are:

1. _____

2. _____

3. _____

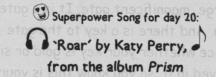

Day 20 affirmation

∞ **Imagination rules: I imagine my life is full of all my great ambitions. I breathe in dreams; I breathe out happiness.** ∞

😊 **Superpower Song for day 20:**
🎧 **'Roar' by Katy Perry,** ♪
from the album *Prism*

Day 21

The Story of Me

Now you've started to challenge your thinking, you can use your power to recreate your life. We can use a garden as a metaphor for changing our life. Maybe you're really happy with how you are creating your life or maybe you'd make a few changes. Think back to the 'garden of your life' from yesterday and maybe add a few more weeds (worries) and a few more seeds (wonders) before doing this visualisation.

SOWING SEEDS OF WONDER FOR YOU AND WEEDING OUT YOUR WORRIES

Start with the magic 3.

Now just imagine you are walking along a path of calm and confidence of happiness and peace.

You feel light and bright as you walk along your special path … There are beautiful flowers around you … little birds singing and squirrels playing. In front of you is a large, magnificent gate. It is a gate that leads you to your own magic garden. And there is a key to the gate … It is magically in your hands now … Notice whether your key is gold or silver or wooden. The key has your name carved in it, so you know this is your gate and your key …

You now enter your special garden. It is a garden of your choice. Notice what flowers, plants, fruits, trees, toys, trampolines and maybe pets are in your magical garden. You notice some weeds in your garden and think it is time to clear them up. You take a rubbish bag and start to collect these weeds. You can imagine that they are your worries or anxieties and your negative thoughts about yourself. Imagine you're pulling those weeds out of your mind, making room for more calm, happy, funny and accepting thoughts.

Anything you want you can plant in this magic garden … You may plant seeds of peace and love … or of joy and happiness … or of brilliance and calmness … or any other qualities you would like to increase in or bring into your life … This is your own magical space. Just spend a few minutes imagining all the lovely things you would like to create in your life.

When you're ready, gently open your eyes and focus on your breathing for a moment.

Power point: With your laser vision, over the next week consider which behaviours or unhelpful thoughts you would like to weed out or let go of and think of two or three habits, behaviours or actions you would like to improve in your life. No time to waste – let's get weeding and seeding the best life possible for right here and now.

DAY TWENTY ONE ☀ POWER POINTS TO REMEMBER

Flick through your journal and remember your positive affirmations and happiness/calm statements. Make a list of positive statements about yourself – e.g., I am unique; a comic genius; amazing at footy; brilliant at ballet; a great mate; gutsy and go for it; or brilliant, confident and bright!

WHAT ARE YOU GROWING IN YOUR BRAIN?

What is the Story of Awesome Me and how great can I make it be?

Get a big piece of paper or whole blank page in your journal, some felt-tip pens or crayons, or even paints, and fill the page with your strengths – words like 'kind', 'fun', 'great swimmer', 'supportive friend', 'quirky', 'arty', 'deep thinker', 'nature/ animal lover', 'good at craft', etc. As Taylor Swift shares: **'Unique and different is the next generation of beautiful.'**

Consider this statement and then finish the following sentence three times.

∞ I LOVE CREATING THE STORY OF ME - I CAN CREATE ANYTHING I WANT TO HAPPEN. I AM AWESOME. THE POSSIBILITIES ARE ENDLESS FOR ME - I CAN DO IT. ∞

Three areas where I can make the Story of Me more awesome are:

1. _____

2. _____

3. _____

I am confident –
I can achieve anything.
I can do it!

Day 21 affirmation

∞ I am confident and awesome. I breathe in confidence; I breathe out possibility. ∞

🎧 Superpower Song for day 21:

🎧 'Shining Star' by Jump5, from *The Lizzie McGuire Movie* ♪

😊 Week 3 inspiration:

'3 tips to boost your confidence',
published on YouTube by TED-Ed - https://youtu.be/l_NYrWqUR40

WEEK FOUR

LET'S GET PHYSICAL – FEEL-GOOD FOOD AND POWER UP WITH EXERCISE

STILL IN ACT TWO

✔ Approach to your innermost cave and facing an ordeal – you've got this!

It is health that is real wealth and not
pieces of gold and silver.

—Mahatma Gandhi

Day 22

Are You Ready to Transform Your Body?

*I*t has been said that something as small as the flutter of a butterfly's wing can ultimately cause a typhoon halfway around the world – chaos theory.

'Wait a minute, what has a butterfly got to do with my body?' I hear you ask. Well, what this means is that the part affects the whole, and every action has a ripple that can travel a long way. Woah, I know – pretty major, and that's why taking responsibility, individually, is such an important and exciting idea, as what you do in life affects everyone else!

We can add to the positive or negative vibes with our thoughts, speech and actions. We know this, but did you know we create vibes by what we eat and how we move? Well, we do. Exercise and food are part of our **power tool kit** because everything affects everything.

The flapping butterfly wings represent small changes to what we eat and how we exercise – our current state – which cause a chain of events leading to large-scale phenomena: us having increased health and well-being. If the butterfly had not flapped its wings, the trajectory of the system might have been vastly different. If you do not create fabulous new vibes by eating feel-good mood foods and taking exercise to get the runner's high, the dancer's buzz or just a great old endorphin flow, how resilient and happy you feel could also be different. There is a good word for this: **holistic**.

If you take notice, there are a lot of butterfly effects in our behaviour. What I mean by this is that there are a lot of micro (small) decisions (eating crisps/sweets every day, skipping games or not drinking water) that we repeat over and over on a daily basis – behaviour that over time leads to very large positive or negative consequences on our well-being.

To look at yourself in a holistic way is looking at each individual part of you as interconnected with the whole of you. We can also look at our own body in this holistic way. Our body is a complex, extraordinary, highly-tuned system, just like the planet we live on, where everything is connected. The flowers need the bees to pollinate them and the bees need the pollen to make honey at the macro (larger) level – it's easy to see how nature is interconnected, and at the micro, individual level, we only have think about the mind–body connection to see a holistic approach makes sense.

You make these small butterfly decisions every day, and usually you make the same choice every time for any particular decision. The choices you make become habits, and habits determine your personality. If you change them, your whole personality changes. You can move from the ordinary world to the extraordinary world with your thinking, and that will make a lasting impression on the rest of your life. Try to push and challenge yourself to do things differently sometimes, to see what happens. You might just see a butterfly effect.

DAY 22: LET'S REVISIT THE MIND/BODY CONNECTION

OK, think of a bright, juicy, zesty lemon. Imagine cutting that lemon open and squeezing the juice into your mouth – wow, it is really sharp as it hits your tongue! This could be the juiciest lemon you've ever tasted … sense that juice squirting into your mouth. Did you notice you started salivating? Everything you do has an effect on you. We told the brain we wanted lemons and it gave us the experience of them in our body!

Trillions of cogs are working in this awesome body of ours, and if one of the cogs is not functioning well, it will have a knock-on effect on another until the whole machine goes out of sync.

Physical movement and regular exercise are good for you. You know this. Who doesn't? And whether it's dancing in your room, playing footy with your mates, a bike ride, a swim in the pool, gymnastics, running or even your walk to school, a little each day goes a long way.

It will make you feel better, happier and stronger. Apart from keeping your muscles, joints, heart and lungs fit, when you exercise your body releases those friendly endorphins. Just like when you think of lemons it makes you salivate, through a chemical response.

Remember – endorphins are happy chemicals, they help reduce stress, increase confidence, help you deal with life's challenges and they help you to fight infection.

The same goes for food – it affects your mood, and who wouldn't want to eat themselves happy? The good news is you can, with all the trappings! The bad news is you can also eat yourself unhappy. Whatever you do raises or lowers your feel-good vibes. Once again, you are in control. No time to lose. Let's get on with it.

During the next seven days we'll be exploring exercise, food and mood, and you'll become your own body coach. We'll celebrate the walks to school, kicking a ball around with your mates or dancing in your room, and we'll tally up the crisps, coke, burgers and sweets and decide if too much of anything can make you feel sick, literally!

EAT Diet Exercise
Body Success
Active Healthy Food
Motivation Living Gym
Sport Life
Joy Fit Optimism

As we've seen, being the director of your life makes sense. You are learning that you are good enough already, and directing your mind so you can look after yourself even more is the way to go. Your true power lies in the knowledge you can do anything you put your mind to. You know exercise is good for you, so let's get moving and build a strong body.

Consider this statement and then finish the following sentence three times.

I FEEL GOOD ABOUT MYSELF –
I AM ENOUGH.

∞ I AM ENOUGH AND I'VE ALWAYS BEEN ENOUGH.
I DON'T COMPARE MYSELF TO OTHERS ANYMORE,
I FEEL GOOD ABOUT MYSELF AND I TAKE ACTIONS
THAT SUPPORT ME – I AM UNSTOPPABLE. ∞

Three mental attitudes I can create to make my mind stronger and feel great about exercising are:

1. _____

2. _____

3. _____

Day 22 affirmation

∞ I believe in myself – I am powerful. I breathe in power;
I breathe out strength. ∞

😺 Superpower Song for day 22:

🎧 'Gonna Fly Now' by Bill Conti, ♪
from the movie *Rocky*

Day 23

The Benefits of Mindful Exercise

Keeping physically healthy is as much about listening to our bodies as it is about running around the track at school. You can develop a really friendly relationship with your body by learning to become more aware of it – by really listening in to it.

INCREASING CALM AND FEEDING YOUR PREFRONTAL CORTEX

Mindful movement is something that can help you awaken to your ever-changing physical sensations. Stretches, simple balances and yoga help to build both physical and mental balance, and in turn these movement challenges help you to grow your awareness and focus your brain.

You have heard of the prefrontal cortex – remember, we talked about it in week one? It's that very important wise-wizard part of the brain, and is the most recently evolved area of the brain. The prefrontal cortex helps us make good decisions, the type of decisions that help us to achieve our goals and organise a life that will make us feel happy and fulfilled.

Yoga and balance exercises can increase calm and mental focus, and thereby help you to have more control over your emotions – the butterfly effect at work!

It is scientifically proven that children who learn to control their own emotional state become more confident and successful, both socially and academically.

—MindUP, the signature program of the Goldie Hawn Foundation

The **power mindset** helps us get good at stuff – it wakes us up to actions that make us feel great, and exercise is part of the power kit.

'What's in it for me?' you might ask. Well, let me tell you – a lot! Check out these researched facts for fun. You have the power to:

- be fitter and healthier
- be more aware of the present moment
- be more confident in teams and with friendships
- be more peaceful and relaxed in body and mind
- be stronger and healthier in your bones and muscles
- be less likely to get diseases such as diabetes
- be more creative and curious

💜 see your self-esteem improve – noticing moods/emotions/body sensations

💜 be calmer, as the symptoms of anxiety and stress reduce

💜 be better able to concentrate, with improved memory function and sense of well-being.

Brilliant – it turns out to be more woah than woe ... Yep, all you need is an open mind to believe in yourself and take up the challenge. Couldn't be easier, hey? I'm not asking you to run a marathon. No. Maybe just get off the bus a couple of stops early and walk the rest of the way to school, or do a bit of routine (practice) exercise a week, and you get all this. Now that's a powerful choice. What's that, you say? You're flapping your wings as we speak!

DAY 23: LET'S GET PHYSICAL – FOR ME, MYSELF AND I

Be positive – think of things you'll stick at, and remember you've got to practice! Why not chat with one of your mates about something you could do together. As always, do the magic 3 to get relaxed. Now put on your thinking cap and have a go at the following:

Write down three ways you can move more, maybe even groove that dancing!

1. _____

2. _____

3. _____

Three actions you can take to get the amazing benefits of more movement:

1. _____

2. _____

3. _____

Be your own body coach. Write down three negative thoughts you're ready to ditch today about your ability and attitude to exercise:

1. _____

2. _____

3. _____

DAY TWENTY THREE ☀ POWER POINTS TO REMEMBER

From today you can choose to start prioritising your happiness. Maybe you can drop some behaviours that aren't good for you – maybe limit your computer screen time or curb your Netflix-binge-worthy shows, and do 30 minutes' exercise instead. What you think you will create.

Consider this statement and then finish the following sentence three times.

I AM STRONG AND I KNOW MY WORTH. AND I KNOW ALL DIAMONDS FACE PRESSURE BEFORE THEY SPARKLE!

∞ WHEN I FEEL GOOD, I ATTRACT GREAT THINGS IN MY LIFE. I REFUSE TO DIM MY POWER OR DOUBT MYSELF. I VALUE MYSELF AND I DO EXERCISE TO SUPPORT MY WELL-BEING. I AM STRONG AND I KNOW MY WORTH. ∞

Three areas I can be firm with myself about creating a healthy, strong body are:

1. _____

2. _____

3. _____

Day 23 affirmation

∞ I am valuable – I rate myself. I let the light of my power shine. I'm strong and kind. I breathe in light; I breathe out kindness. ∞

😊 Superpower Song for day 23:

🎧 'Keep On Movin' by Five, 🎵
from the album *Invincible*

Day 24

Inhale Wonder, Exhale Worry

There are loads of amazing and gentle yoga workshops online that you can try for free – either ask your parents to help, or search Google and YouTube yourself for 'gentle yoga for beginners' or 'yoga balances for beginners'. Try some of the balancing exercises to see how they feel. Could you commit to doing just five or ten minutes three times a week to improve your brain's focus, balance and strength?

Try walking with a book on your head. Keep the book balanced without touching it. Create a mini obstacle course to make the exercise harder. Try this on your own, or for a laugh with your mum, dad, brother, sister or friend!

Try not to laugh – you might as it's surprisingly hard not to!

When you get balanced, be aware of the constantly changing physical sensations. This simple exercise, practised regularly, will make you a balance ninja, strengthen your tummy and leg muscles, and increase your brainpower – which means focus and intelligence.

Mind-bending fact: we don't get good at stuff if we are afraid of looking daft! Remember, the worry mindset can seriously hold us back.

Let's take a look at a simple yoga pose.

Yoga teaches non-judgment and non-competition towards oneself and one another. It increases self-acceptance too. This all means it can make you feel happier with who you are and be more open and less jealous or competitive with others. I know, we don't like to admit feeling this way, but heigh-ho, you've just got to let go …

THE TREE

Try this simple balance, and all the while really listen in to your body and its sensations. Don't worry if you wobble, just notice and try not to judge. Remember to be aware of your thoughts, and be kind to yourself.

⭐ Stand with your feet together and your arms by your sides.

⭐ Warm up the ankles by circling first one foot, then the other.

⭐ Steady your body and distribute your weight equally on both feet.

⭐ Raise your left leg, bend the knee and place the sole on the inner side of your right thigh.

⭐ Fix your eyes on one point and find your balance.

⭐ Inhale, raise your arms over your head, bring your palms together and stretch your arms, shoulders and chest upwards.

⭐ Stretch your whole body from top to bottom, without losing balance or moving your feet.

⭐ Hold the position for five breaths.

⭐ Exhale slowly and release your arms and left leg down to the starting position.

⭐ Repeat on the other side.

How did it feel?

Was one side different to the other? Did you resist? Can you commit to doing this balance every day for a week? You will really notice how much easier it becomes every day. Practice, practice, practice – build your power muscles.

KEEP CALM & BE BALANCED

DAY TWENTY FOUR ☀ POWER POINTS TO REMEMBER

Working out is just another superpower in the arsenal that is your radiant health. Keeping our energy flowing with exercise makes us feel great all round. We saw earlier the benefits of exercise: amongst other things, it fuels our happy hormones, makes us clearer and helps us feel more confident. Caring for your body makes sense. As always, it's consistency and practice that get the best results. You are worth it, so commit to doing a workout a few times a week.

KEEP CALM & DO YOGA

I AM STRONG, CALM AND BALANCED, AND I CAN DO IT!

Consider this statement and then finish the following sentence three times.

∞ I MOVE MY BODY AND LOVE FEELING HEALTHY.
I AM HAPPY WITH THE CHANGES I AM MAKING: I FEEL STRONGER,
CALMER AND GLOWING WITH GOOD HEALTH. ∞

Three areas where the butterfly of exercise increases my feelings of well-being are:

1. _____

2. _____

3. _____

Day 24 affirmation

∞ I am balanced and calm. I breathe in calm; I breathe out balance. ∞

😊 Superpower Song for day 24:
🎧 'Hall of Fame' by The Script, ♪
featuring Will.i.am, from the album #3

Day 25

Coaching Power – Create a Plan

For the next power, find a friend to buddy (coach) up with so you can support and coach each other.

Let's make a plan. **Just do it**, as our friend Nike tells us!

We have no time to lose – our physical agility depends on us and, well, the benefits rock. Look – you've got this, just get on your thinking cap and then let's break your goal down into small chunks. Listen, all heroes reckon it's a good idea to stay fit, and going for gold calls for a bit of planning, so let's spend five minutes brainstorming your ideas around the exercise you want to do and how often you'll do it.

💡 _____

💡 _____

💡 _____

💡 _____

💡 _____

It's a good idea to ask a friend to do the following exercise with you; that way you get to motivate each other.

Dreams are free. Goals have a cost. While you can daydream for free, goals don't come without a price. Time, Effort, Sacrifice, and Sweat. How will you pay for your goals?

—Usain Bolt

157

POWER COACHING EXERCISE

Chat these points through with a friend:

- What is your **mindful exercise plan**? Be honest about whether these are things that you can easily put in place. Try to be realistic so that you can stick to your plan – you don't want to feel you've failed just because your goals were too difficult to achieve. Talk to your **buddy coach** about what's possible.

- How will you commit to your plan? How will you make time? Perhaps think about how focusing on the benefits will help to motivate you.

- When will you start? Avoid negative 'self-chatter' – it could hold you back. Clear your head of the little voice that says (if not today, then in a few days), 'I'm too tired,' or 'Just missing one won't hurt!' Put a start date down today in your journal.

- Why focus on your goal? Create positive self-belief – what's in it for you? What will be different when you commit to your healthier living idea?

- Where will you place your reminders to keep you on track – e.g., stickers or a memory wall in school or a daily activity log to record your success? Note down how it makes you feel. Fix times to chat to your buddy coach about your progress or challenges each week.

- What might you stand to lose if you commit to this plan – e.g., sweets, electronic games, extra time in bed, treats, television?

Listen, I know it can be challenging but remember every accomplishment starts with the desire to change. It will also be great connecting with your mate and supporting each other. Spend around 30 minutes each way.

If you fall short, don't give up, just start again. As J. K. Rowling says: 'Failure taught me things about myself I could have learnt no other way. I discovered I had a strong will and more discipline than I had suspected.'

Listen, this change in thinking is radical – we are moving into a world where we love and accept our body just as it is. Remember, everything is connected and when we have unkind thoughts about our body we are basically diminishing the light of our power. Making healthy changes makes you feel good about yourself. It's time to trust in yourself – life is what you make it. You have the power to love and accept yourself and your body, just as you are. Remember – where attention goes energy flows, so think you can change and view the world through the eyes of your wonder power!

I TAKE ONE DAY AT A TIME.
I'VE GOT THIS – I ACCEPT MYSELF.

Consider this statement and then finish the following sentence three times.

∞ I LOVE MY BODY – I ACCEPT MYSELF JUST AS I AM. EVERYTHING STARTS WITH HOW I FEEL ABOUT MYSELF. I CAN DO GREAT THINGS – I AM THE CREATOR OF MY STRONG HEALTHY BODY. ∞

Three attitudes I can have to feel good about myself and accept myself are:

1. _____

2. _____

3. _____

Day 25 affirmation

∞ I am patient – the results I want happen one day at a time. I breathe in patience; I breathe out glowing health. ∞

😊 Superpower Song for day 25:

🎧 'The Climb' by Miley Cyrus, ♪
from *Hannah Montana: The Movie*

WEEK FOUR – HEROIC HARRY TO THE RESCUE

Week four: Inner cave and ordeal

Harry had to admit the thought of standing up to Snake was dead thrilling.

Tom, all animated, was like, 'Come on, mate, you don't have to take it anymore. He's such an idiot, always hurling insults at you. Stand up to him, it'll feel great. I'll be with you – safety in numbers. Maybe the muppet will even try something down the track. That would be a brilliant place for you to flex your "damn it – no more" muscles, they all think you're a regular hero there. You've got the power! Boss lad.' Tom smiled. They both laughed.

'Don't you know it, mate,' said Harry, laughing. 'Give me a minute to get my kit and we'll get going,' he said, praying: *'Will it be, well, possible to square up to Snake? Come on, God, my mum's always saying "***the universe has your back***" – please let it have mine today. I am so sick of the grisly punishments Snake thinks he can dole out, I hate him – he's a real coward, a real loser.'* He started to breathe and felt peace in his heart, the type he felt singing in the choir at church on Sunday.

Looking back, he remembered it began almost instantly, when Snake joined their school last year. He just started pushing Harry around. Harry had been really low after the divorce, and felt insecure – his head was all over the place at the time – but he felt fine now.

Then, with ninja insight, he realised: Snake took his sadness for weakness. The truth was his head was done in – he didn't want to get into a fight, so he just tried to ignore it. Until that moment he'd never thought of it, but – he gasped as he realised – he'd just got into the groove of playing the role of being bullied, and when he worried he felt worse. He said to himself, 'No more!'

Later, when they arrived at the track, like clockwork Snake started with the insults. Jonesy hadn't arrived so he was taking the opportunity to pounce on his prey.

The knot in Harry's stomach tightened and with pulse-pounding courage he looked Snake in the eye and firmly said, 'STOP. I want you to STOP right now. STOP.'

Gobsmacked, Snake did a double take. 'What, you little squirt, don't tell me what to do, lad,' he said, raising his voice. A crowd started to gather with all the commotion.

'STOP. I want you to STOP right now. STOP.' Harry repeated it calmly and firmly. Snake was getting more flustered as, the truth is, there's nothing funny or mean to say about 'Stop.'

'God, that was scary,' thought Harry, but he also noticed a lot of the group were standing behind him now.

Then Jonesy called, 'What's all this then, lads?'

'Nothing, Sir. Just saying the new tracks are boss,' said Harry, feeling that powerful peace again and taking control. Again, to Snake's surprise.

Tom patted him on the back and whispered, 'You were the boss. Safe territory for now, mate, and at least he knows he can't mug you off again without a fight. You were great the way you didn't let him get in your face.' Harry felt calm and this new air of confidence was filling him with good vibes. He knew there would be more to come, but he felt ready.

Paula thinks:

Harry reflected in his cave, making the link that Snake had started bullying him when he felt vulnerable around his parents' divorce. He has emerged with the confidence and courage to face his ordeal and stand up to Snake. He's ditching worrying over the past and thinking he's not good enough. The coaching exercises and the garden of life will have really helped Harry as they invite you to reflect, which often brings insight – for example, when the bullying began.

He has reclaimed his power and believed enough in himself to put a stop to his biggest fear, and has stood up to Snake for the first time. He behaves assertively and, like any good Jedi, he does not abuse his power. He is choosing to believe anything is possible through his mindful, compassionate and courageous approach. He is also calling on his faith and anchoring in the powerful feeling of peace he gets in church – feeling supported and loved by an unseen hand of God, which connects him directly to his spirit – empowering him even more.

Harry will be getting lots of happy hormones from all the exercise he is doing. We learnt earlier that his mum likes to make sure he eats well and has healthy smoothies, which will also be helping. Remember, the holistic approach looks at all the ways we can improve our well-being on all fronts – mind, body and spirit.

It is lovely that Harry is really beginning to value himself. He sees he is part of a team and is connected, and feels grateful. He feels confident, happy and calm and is transforming his fear – he is awesome and deserves to celebrate.

WEEK FOUR – WHO KNEW OLIVIA? GO GIRL!

Week four: Approach to your innermost cave

Oliva dashed up the stairs and clicked on her FaceTime. 'Is that my princess?' her dad asked with a grin. He was a soldier on tour, but would soon be based at home to be with her. 'Only two more weeks, gorgeous.' He laughed. 'What's happening your end?'

'I need you, Dad. I choked on my maths test – it was like my brain just up and left my body. Total nightmare. I've also got the *Strictly* competition and Katie is certain we'll win!'

'Wow – slow down! I'm guessing choked means around 65%?' He smiled.

'68%, actually, but you know maths is my best subject, and to do physics and engineering, I need to stay at the top with it,' she said.

He laughed again. 'You'll ace it when you need to, in three years! Now tell me more about *Strictly*. What makes Katie think you guys could win, apart from the fact you're amazingly talented, of course?' he asked, grinning. His positivity was contagious.

She laughed, gushing out the evidence: 'We've been asked to open the show. Everyone keeps saying we're great.' Slowing down, she said, 'But ... Dad, I'm so nervous and we have an audience rehearsal in hour ...'

'OK kiddo, you need your head in the game. The evidence is you can do it, but your monkey mind is telling you you'll make a mistake, forget your moves, go red and the world will end. It won't, lovely, nervousness is natural – it gives you the adrenaline boost to perform under pressure. I tell my squad that, and it's true. So, Private Chambers [that's Olivia's surname], get out there and strut your stuff – you can do this!' He beamed his order.

'Love you, Dad – you're right. I've got to get down the hall and "strut my stuff". Bye.' She saluted, smiling, and shouted, 'I love you!' before clicking FaceTime off.

Livy felt a bit nervous, but Katie was absolutely radiant with confidence and excitement. 'Gosh, you look so happy, Katie – aren't you worried we'll make a mistake in front of the audience?' she asked.

'A little, but all great performers make the odd mistake – we can't let it define us. The show must go on, it will be alright on the night, darling … Come on, you know the drill, we've trained for this – let's go out and enjoy it! Oh, that's our cue.' Katie said, hugging Livy.

The rehearsal went amazingly, and Olivia felt awesome. Katie was smiling at her. 'See – I told you you'd be excellent. You were, we both were! This is our first step on the road to international dance stardom, Livy, drink in the moment!' Katie hugged her again and Livy, feeling really grateful, thought, 'Katie is the best friend.'

Paula thinks:

Olivia's confidence has grown and her can-do attitude is growing. She has a good-vibe tribe around her who support her. Olivia is mastering her worries (the dragons) with practice; she knows they'll pop up breathing fire-thoughts of doom and gloom again.

She also knows they are just thoughts, and thoughts are not facts. She has slain her metaphorical dragon for now and is enjoying the rewards of more confidence and happiness. She has faced her fear of public performance and feels a new person, with happier vibes and more contented thinking and feeling. Best of all, she is trusting in herself and her dreams.

She is growing in resilience and developing more self-acceptance and compassion. This is making her realise she is enough just as she is, and there is no need to compare herself anymore – she just wants to be the best she can be. Doing the exercises around thinking will have helped her understand that she can grow new ideas in the garden of her life, and she can take control of her thinking to improve her sense of happiness, confidence or relaxation.

All of her dancing will be giving her endorphin boosts, which, essentially, as you know, just make you feel so much better. Being mindful of her eating will also support her continued success on the road to well-being and increased confidence and happiness.

She is grateful for her family and friends and feels excited about her achievement. Go Olivia! **You've got the power!**

Day 26

Who Wouldn't Want to Eat Themselves Happy?

Today we are going to be all over your recipes for success. We've all heard the old saying, 'You are what you eat.' Right? But did you know the mind–body connection is activated by our food choices too? Food affects our biology and our biology affects our psychology. Put simply, food affects our brain! The butterfly effect again ...

Fancying junk food more than is healthy for you may drive your parents nuts and, although we don't like it, let's get hardcore over it – they've got a point here! Your eating habits may be less than stellar, and don't assume you'll eventually have the same eating repertoire as the God of Healthy Eating, because the chances are you won't! The truth is studies show you carry over your eating habits into adulthood, so it's best to deal with them now.

Good eating habits aren't so pesky, either, they can rock – helping you be stronger, more alert and just much better on the inside. Remember the old saying: garbage in, garbage out ... Take a shifty at these benefits of eating well – there's no garbage here. You will:

1. be in a better **mood** – if you're happy and you know it, clap your hands!

2. have an improved **memory** – ninja recall in exams!

3. have a healthy **bodyweight** for your age and height

4. become an activist of the **wellness revolution**! Go you ...

5. avoid **obesity** and **type 2 diabetes** – boom!

6. feel **healthier** and eat yourself **happy**! What's not to like?

7. have stronger **bones** – even the funny one!

8. have healthy **teeth** – yay, less dentist!

SCRAP THE CRAP – DIVING STRAIGHT IN!

The food we eat affects how we feel, and therefore how we act. Whatever you're munching your way through, it makes sense to be mindful. Crap isn't the nicest word, but we all know what it means, don't we?

Carbonated drinks

Refined sugar

Artificial flavourings

Processed foods

Look, none of us would choose to feel low, and it's great we can feed ourselves with food that makes us feel great, but first we need to scrap the crap. I know – it's nearly impossible. Refined sugar and processed foods are everywhere, but we can make some power choices. Here's the low-down on why it's worth making some cool fuel choices in the future:

Carbonated drinks are linked to tooth decay because they are acidic and damage comes from their sugar content and additives. Sorry, you can't get away with the zero-sugar kind: research shows diet versions aren't any better!

Refined sugar doesn't have any nutritional benefits, and this type of sugar is absorbed quickly into our bloodstream and also leaves quickly, causing blood-sugar levels to spike. It is also known to contribute to diseases like type 2 diabetes. Many processed foods contain refined sugar, but some obvious ones are cakes, biscuits, cereals and ready meals.

Artificial additives and flavourings in foods are classed as 'anti-nutrients'. Remember when we chatted about stress hormones killing happy hormones? Well, these are similar as they can rob or cancel out vital nutrients our bodies need.

Processed foods often contain refined sugars, and are high in salt, artificial flavourings, and saturated and trans fats. It is best to try to stick with a whole-foods diet and consume foods in their most natural form, where possible. Remember, the key is moderation – we spoke about aiming for an 80/20 ratio, with 80 on the healthy side being the power choice here.

HOW CAN I MAKE THE CUT FOR ME, MYSELF AND I?

Carbonated drinks: how can I cut down and what will I replace them with? Please say water!

1. _____

2. _____

3. _____

Refined sugar: this is the one hidden everywhere, remember! Cut it quick ...

1. _____

2. _____

3. _____

Artificial flavourings: there's a happy-hormones killer on the loose – I refuse:

1. _____

2. _____

3. _____

Processed foods: making food choices to fire up my power. What can I do now?

1. _____

2. _____

3. _____

DAY TWENTY SIX ☀ POWER POINTS TO REMEMBER

Our bodies are intelligent, and they are very powerful too. If we cut ourselves, the body naturally heals the cut without us telling it to! The body is always working to keep us healthy, and if we eat food high in nutrients we make the job easier for it; naturally, the opposite applies here too. To take care of our body we need to be mindful about what we put in it to avoid lowering our immune system and feeling low. In a nutshell, that's why eating healthy is so important.

I NOURISH MY BODY WITH HEALTHY FOODS; I FEEL POWERFUL.

Consider this statement and then finish the following sentence three times.

∞ I LOVE MY BODY AND FILLING IT WITH NUTRITIOUS FOOD TO INCREASE MY POWER. EATING THE RIGHT FOODS MAKES ME FEEL FIT, HEALTHY AND GOOD ABOUT MYSELF. ∞

Three ways I can feel more fit, healthy and good about myself with food are:

1. _____

2. _____

3. _____

Day 26 affirmation

∞ I am healthy and I feel good about myself. I breathe in happiness; I breathe out positive energy. ∞

😊 Superpower Song for day 26:

🎧 'Shake It Off' by Taylor Swift, ♪
from the album *1989*

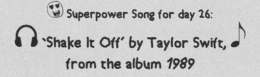

Day 27

Eat Happy-Hormone Brain Food

Thinking about what we eat is clearly part of our recipe for success. No, you don't have to go completely plant-based, which is really trendy at the moment, but of course it's okay if you do. About 95% of the 'good-mood' neurotransmitter serotonin is produced in the gut, and a deficiency can have a direct impact on well-being, resulting in symptoms such as low mood, anxiety and poor sleep. Here's a list of some of the top foods to boost serotonin levels:

1. Berries – love strawberries, raspberries and blue berries – no complaints here

2. Beans – yes, even baked beans, and who doesn't love Mexican, arriba, arriba …

3. Dark chocolate – that's my kind of food!

4. Fish – maybe not battered with chips – well, just occasionally, good for the soul …

5. Herbal teas – green, chamomile, mint, chia – decisions, decisions

6. Spinach – apparently good for muscles, according to Popeye!

7. Whole fruits – including an apple a day keeps the doctor away

8. Turkey or tofu – Christmas dinner sorted

9. Planting happiness with sunflower or pumpkin seeds

10. Go nuts with almonds and walnuts

11. Asparagus – not sure what to say!

12. Pineapple – Sponge Bob Square Pants, and all that

13. Cottage cheese – unlucky for some!

So next time you're feeling a bit down, why not snack on some of the above foods – they are way ahead of the others in terms of boosting serotonin levels and brain power, so they're a pick-me-up too. What's not to like?

Every kid in every school no matter their background, deserves to learn the basics about food – where it comes from, how to cook it and how it affects their bodies. These life skills are as important as reading and writing, but they've been lost over the past few generations. We need to bring them back and bring up our kids to be streetwise about food.

—Jamie Oliver

DAY 27: POWERFUL CHOICES FOR ME, MYSELF AND I

Put your thinking cap on, and have a go at the following:

Three fuel (food) choices I am good at:

1. _____

2. _____

3. _____

Three fuel (food) choices I'd like to be good at:

1. _____

2. _____

3. _____

Three fuel (food) choices that are not so good for my health:

1. _____

2. _____

3. _____

DAY 27: MINDFUL EATING

Power practice: it is funny how often we eat without noticing what is happening as we do. We may taste the first bite and the last bite, but the eating in the middle seems to go unnoticed. We call this behaving on autopilot, where we do things subconsciously without thinking. This means we

Don't rush

Consider the source

Drink Water

Love what you eat

Question what you eat

Enjoy the Experience

Avoid distractions

don't experience all the loveliness of, for example, a bar of chocolate! By applying mindfulness to our everyday routines, like eating, we can develop a greater appreciation of our food and lives.

This helps us develop a 'beginner mind', which really means acting like it is the first time we have seen, experienced or heard something. Having a beginner mind can also be described as being more curious and approaching things with awe and excitement or trepidation.

With mindful eating we connect with our senses and mindfully enjoy what we are eating more. When we are more aware of the process of eating, whether it is with chocolate, nuts, fruit or an entire meal, we can experience more satisfaction.

Do we think mindful eating could help us make healthier choices when eating?

Just like they say, 'You are what you think,' they say, 'You are what you eat' too. This simply means the healthy and wholesome foods you eat make you feel healthy and happy. I want to be as inclusive as possible, embracing all cuisines and cultures. One size does not fit all in the food department, and an anti-anything agenda won't help anyone. All different kinds of food, including sweets and cakes, are fine in moderation if your overall eating is balanced and healthy.

Consider this statement and then finish the following sentence three times.

EATING LOVELY, NUTRITIOUS, GOOD-MOOD FOOD IS A RECIPE FOR SUCCESS!

∞ I CHOOSE TO EAT HEALTHY NUTRITIOUS FOOD, AND I FEEL GREAT ABOUT MYSELF. I TAKE GOOD CARE OF MY BODY. MY ENERGY IS VIBRANT. I DITCH SLUGGISH, LOW-MOOD FOOD. ∞

Three good-mood foods I can eat more and create a recipe for success are:

1. _____

2. _____

3. _____

Day 27 affirmation

∞ I am vibrant and healthy. I breathe in sunshine; I breathe out freedom. ∞

Superpower Song for day 27:

🎧 'Walking on Sunshine' by Katrina and the Waves, ♪
from the album *Walking on Sunshine*

Day 28

Mindful Eating and Hydration

When our bodies are calm and peaceful we are much more likely to absorb the nutrients from what we are eating. Slow and deliberate eating supports good digestion. Mindful eating helps you to tune into your body and noticing helps you know when you are hungry, thirsty or full. Did you know people often eat when actually they are thirsty, and that keeping hydrated curbs your appetite?

WHY DRINK WATER?

1. Lose Weight
2. Healthy Skin
3. Fights Infection
4. Rids of Body Toxins
5. Healthy Heart

6. Prevents Pains
7. Boosts Energy
8. Prevents Constipation
9. reduces cancer risk
10. Improves productivity

SMART VISUALISATION

Imagine a huge buffet table is in front of you. It has lots of lovely foods and drinks which are really healthy for you. Think of the foods that you really enjoy and imagine yourself eating a delicious strawberry or other nutritious foods.

Can you imagine three or four other healthy foods which will support your healthy growth and add to feelings of happiness and well-being? Just rest in your mind now and notice the foods that pop up for you, which are good for you – maybe a carrot or corn, an apple or banana – just listen to your body and see what comes up for you.

Yum – a chocolate meditation!

Take a piece of chocolate – maybe a type you have never tried before, it could be organic or fair trade. Before unwrapping the chocolate look at it, notice the colours and shine of the wrapper. Notice how the wrapping feels as you unfold it.

Look at the chocolate: what colours and shapes do you notice? Inhale the aroma of the chocolate and let it sweep over you. Take a small piece of it. Look at it as it rests on your hand and let your eyes drink it in. Maybe you notice your taste buds reacting.

Now bring it up to your mouth and notice how your hand knows where to position it. Can you hold it on your tongue and let it melt? Notice the temptation to chew it – does the taste change as you move it to different parts of the tongue?

Did the chocolate taste better than normal?

We are often so busy eating our way through, we don't notice how much taste is in it ... Or maybe we just notice the first and the last taste.

Remember, mindfulness is about bringing awareness to the normal, routine things we do in life. Can you think of other routines where you could apply mindfulness – maybe brushing your teeth or chatting to a friend? Mindfulness helps us really listen, too. We don't need to fix things; we are just there listening to our friend, which is very powerful.

DAY TWENTY EIGHT ☼ POWER POINTS TO REMEMBER

Remember – your body is powerful, in fact it is a miracle. We know the brain has amazing superpowers, but did you know it is composed of 80% water, and that's why drinking lots of water improves our sense of well-being? Hydration supports us in managing any stresses or worries we have. With all this healthy eating, remember to swill it all down with a great attitude of thinking – 'Drinking at least eight glasses of water a day keeps my body and mind healthy and fit.'

I FILL MY BODY WITH
GOOD-MOOD FOOD. I DRINK
PLENTY OF WATER AND
I FEEL GREAT!

Consider this statement and then finish the following sentence three times.

∞ EATING WHOLESOME FOODS AND DRINKING PLENTY OF WATER HELPS ME BE MORE KIND, LOVING AND CONNECTED TO MY BODY. I FEEL SO HEALTHY AND WHOLE, I CHOOSE GOOD-MOOD FOOD AND I DRINK PLENTY OF WATER. ∞

Three ways I can remember to drink more water and enhance my mood are:

1. _____

2. _____

3. _____

Day 28 affirmation

∞ I look after my body, I connect to it and create radiant well-being. I breathe in awareness; I breathe out connection. ∞

😊 Superpower Song for day 28:

🎧 'Beautiful' by Bazzi, featuring Camila Cabello, ♪ from the album *Cosmic*

Week 4 inspiration: 'Science of Happiness', published on YouTube by Life Noggin - https://youtu.be/B19g3oXTD5I

WEEK FIVE

THE ROOTS OF RESILIENCE AND THE WINGS OF FREEDOM

ACT THREE – THE RETURN

- ✔ Reward (seizing the treasure)
- ✔ The road back
- ✔ Resurrection
- ✔ Returning with the elixir

The main thing that you have to remember
on this journey is, just be nice to everyone
and always smile.

—Ed Sheeran

ACT THREE – THE RETURN

Reward (seizing the treasure): And the 'you're-awesome' award goes to you. The crowds roar … you are a hero – you've overcome your challenge and you're transformed with courage and compassion. You are ultimately transformed forever, emerging from your battle as a stronger person – **you've got the power**, the secret, the knowledge and the insight. Your treasure is the achievement of inner change. No time to lose, though – we must quickly put celebrations aside and prepare for the last leg of our journey.

The road back: It's time to leave the special world behind and return to your ordinary world. I know you've got the power, and it feels great. You can show everyone you've got this, and it feels good. But the hero's journey is not yet over: you still have to put your knowledge to the test and experience the living of your goal. Remember, with great power comes great knowledge – so don't be surprised if at this stage there comes a moment in which you must choose between your own greater good and the greater good of the planet!

Resurrection: The stakes are at the highest – all of your old demons will pop up to challenge you – but you've got this. Now is the time to let your training kick in, all the lessons you've learnt – this is the climax: you must have your final and most dangerous encounter. You are at a new beginning with new insights, enlightened to new ways to live in the world. You realise the power has always been within you, and this represents the final death of your worry-ego thoughts. This is a critical point for you. Your passion is ignited and your soul is ready to rise to new heights of acceptance, confidence, kindness and happiness. Your change will change the world for good – remember the butterfly effect.

Returning with the elixir: This is the final stage of your hero's journey. You have changed in miraculous ways and you have superpowers to ignite well-being with effortless ease. Now is the time to implement the changes in your daily life and use the lessons to heal the wounds of your old thinking. You have transformed one area of your life and have the elixir for change in other areas. You have grown as a person from worry to wonder, you've learnt many things, faced many fears, and we love you. We celebrate the start of your new life. Use your elixir of love, wisdom, knowledge and freedom to continue to support yourself, your friends and your family, and create great change in the world.

Ultimately, you, our amazing hero, will return to where you started, but things will clearly never be the same again. Enjoy your celebration, self-realisation or an end to worry, let your change, transformation and success light your way on future missions. You are the leader of your life and you can continue to train your brain to create the life you want.

Day 29

Bouncing Back

Everything we've been practising has been strengthening our resilience.

OK, let's get stuck in. Get an elastic band and hold each end of the elastic in your hands, pull your hands apart and see how the elastic stretches. Let go of one end and the elastic bounces back to its original size. In some ways you are just like that – life's events stretch you, but whatever bad times you go through, like the band, you can always bounce back again. The ability to bounce back or have the capacity to recover quickly from difficulties is called **resilience**. A key fact with resilient people is that they have strong mental toughness.

There is a lot to get stressed about in life, so building your mental muscles is essential. What with unrealistic expectations, exams, exposure to violence, no down time, pressure to achieve, too much electronic-game time, cyberbullying – even trolling, normal bullying or poverty – you can see why developing mental toughness is a must!

In life there will be times when we feel overwhelmed and whilst it would be amazing if we could answer 'yes' to all of the following questions all of the time, sometimes we can't. Yes, I know it's a bit of a blow. However, the great news is that practising building our mental toughness will really help us get back to balance more quickly and tick a big fat 'yes' next to all of them.

- ✓ Do I feel safe?

- ✓ Am I encouraged to do my best?

- ✓ If there is a problem, am I able to talk things over?

- ✓ Are family/school rules simple and easy to understand?

- ✓ Do I feel treated fairly?

- ✓ Do I feel supported?

- ✓ Do I think people are mostly kind and fair?

- ✓ Do I get opportunities to be helpful or volunteer in the community?

- ✓ Do I have time for my favourite hobbies?

- ✓ Do I feel happy?

- ✓ Do I get positive feedback on my work?

- ✓ Do I know what to do if I am being bullied or hurt?

- ✓ Am I encouraged to try new things?

- ✓ Am I encouraged to follow my interests?

DAY 29: MENTAL TOUGHNESS FOR ME, MYSELF AND I

What situations do you think you need more resilience in? Jot down three.

1. _____

2. _____

3. _____

What you've written above may appear like big obstacles, so it's best to make a plan. Let's think how you can take control of your thoughts and emotions to help you. Self-regulation is brilliant, it puts you in control. Maybe you can imagine yourself being awesome and fearless in the situation. Mental rehearsal isn't just for sports people – it's for you too! Thinking about the last 28 days, what can you do to help yourself feel hyped or buzzing to smash your challenging situations?

1. _____

2. _____

3. _____

Think of it like learning a language – you have to practise speaking it to know you're getting good at it. If you want to get faster on the track, you need to practise with fast people who test your ability. Remember – it's natural to feel overwhelmed by things that stretch you, but if you make a plan and break down which bits you are good at you'll feel much better, and then you can just focus on the bits that are freaking you out.

Whatever you have looming in the not-so-distant future, planning helps. As a teacher, I see people ignore the 80% talent they have and put all their worries into the 20% they think they'll never be able to do. Yep, you've got it, they then act surprised and shocked when they nail it. How many times have you worried yourself dizzy about something and then found it was nowhere near as bad as you had thought? Be honest, I am guessing a lot!

When we dare to dream big, the possibility of failure sneaks in beside it. That's why dreaming can feel like a risky business – the possibility of it not going our way can literally stop us even giving it a go. Sometimes we worry our achievements are a fluke and we're unworthy, that somehow beneath the success we're not sure we deserve it. But that's not true, it's just fear – **F**alse **E**vidence **A**ppearing **R**eal – and our way of trying to protect ourselves from possible failure. This is quite depressing and can chip away at our self-esteem, so better to give it a go and take a chance on success.

I DARE TO DREAM BIG – THIS IS MY LIFE AND I CREATE MY REALITY

Consider this statement and then finish the following sentence three times.

∞ I BELIEVE IN MYSELF – I CAN DO GREAT THINGS. I RISE TO THE CHALLENGES IN MY LIFE, AND I AM CONFIDENT AND STRONG. I'VE GOT THIS; I CAN DO GREAT THINGS. ∞

Three areas I am not saying 'yes' to success in are:

1. _____

2. _____

3. _____

Day 29 affirmation

∞ I can make my dreams come true – I believe in myself.
I breathe in possibility; I breathe out dreams. ∞

😍 Superpower Song for day 29:
🎧 'Don't Give Up' by Bruno Mars and *Sesame Street* ♪

Day 30

Thoughts Aren't Facts

Without realising it you've probably had thousands of thoughts which are not facts. Thoughts are just that – thoughts – and thoughts are OK.

Sometimes we have attack thoughts which make us feel unsafe. When this happens, it's good to remember **you've got the power**. We all get times when we feel fear, worry or doubt, or we are ill and feel vulnerable. That's OK, it's perfectly normal. When it happens, though, our true power lies in trying to witness these thoughts and not attaching to them as true.

If I think my hopes and wishes won't work out and life's a mess, I tend to think of my power as love and remember that I can access that loving kindness within me. Seeing with love helps me see I am not separate and alone. I remember that with the power of love I am connected and safe. This helps me feel good and safe, and I know the power of self-compassion and kindness nurtures and supports me.

Chatting with a friend or on your own, try to remember a time you achieved something you thought you couldn't:

⭐ I smashed my comfort zone when I _____

_____

_____

_____

and a time when you thought something and realised it was not true – e.g., you thought you didn't like sweetcorn but you tried it and you did. Or you thought someone ignored you in the street and they were RUDE, but it turned out they had earphones in and it wasn't personal – they just didn't hear you; they literally had other things on their mind, like music!

⭐ My thoughts weren't facts when I _____

_____

_____

_____

DAY 30: MY SAFE-SPACE MEDITATION

Close your eyes and relax. Take a few deep breaths. Now you see in your imagination that there is a magical door in front of you. Somehow you realise that behind the door is your very own special place.

This place can be any place that you want – a place that is calm, relaxing and feels very, very good to you. It can be an ocean; a desert; an island; a forest; the inside of a castle; a cave; on the moon; a star; a planet far, far away or a simple closet under the stairs. It is the first image that comes to you when you hear the words 'special place'.

Now, quietly walk up to the door and place your hand on the doorknob. As you open the door, your special place will unfold before you and you will be free to enter. On the count of three: one ... two ... three. Open the door and step across the threshold into your special place. There it is before your eyes!

What do you see before you? Know that all of this place is your own creation. If you would like to add a tree, a rock, an animal friend, a flower, a star, anything at all – it is up to you. Practise adding a special item to your place. Beautiful! Now practise making it disappear. It is all in your power – you decide what is allowed into your special place. Everything in this place is created by you. No one can enter or exit without your permission. You create every bit of it! What sounds do you hear? You can add other sounds if you would like that will make it more real and fun for you!

Now find a comfortable spot to lie down in your special place. Just relax for a few minutes, taking in the view around you, listening to what is happening in your special place. Know that this place is entirely complete and whole. You are complete and enough in your special place. Breathe into your heart and connect fully with feelings of relaxation. Breathe through your heart centre ... pause ... relax. Let go of the outside world that is beyond this place. Relax. Let go ... Beautiful! Let yourself feel an inner smile for a few breaths. Know that you can return here whenever you like. Now it is time to leave. Gently get up and walk back to the door; pause to look over your shoulder for another glimpse of your special place, knowing that you can return in any moment. Taking two deep breaths in, you can open your eyes when you are ready.

DAY THIRTY ☀ POWER POINTS TO REMEMBER

As we've just seen from the last example, sometimes our thoughts are the opposite of the truth. It can be tricky to free our mind and choose to see peace instead of conflict, or wonder instead of worry. Meditation helps here – whatever is happening on the outside, we can choose to anchor ourselves in peace and stillness by connecting to our breathing. This can help us to remember thoughts are not facts. Sometimes it's hard to leave the prison of negative thinking. If you feel stuck, get support from a parent, teacher or mate.

Consider this statement and then finish the following sentence three times.

I TRUST MYSELF AND KNOW IT
IS SAFE TO ASK FOR HELP.

∞ I KNOW THOUGHTS ARE NOT FACTS AND THAT THINKING AFFECTS FEELING. I AM SAFE. I TRUST MYSELF TO CREATE MY WORLD WITH KINDNESS, EVEN WHEN IT FEELS TOUGH. ∞

Three areas where I can be my own best friend with my thinking are:

1. _____

2. _____

3. _____

Day 30 affirmation

∞ I am safe and loving, and I create my world with kindness.
I breathe in safety; I breathe out love. ∞

😊 Superpower Song for day 30:
🎧 'Try Everything' by Shakira, ♪
from the movie *Zootopia*

Day 31

It's All in the Wiring ...

Feelings: everyone has them, right? They change moment by moment, and we can have more than one feeling at a time. Feelings aren't right or wrong, and it's OK to feel what we feel. **How are you feeling today?** Maybe happy, kind, sad, proud, shy, frustrated, silly, surprised, sneaky, nervous, embarrassed, grumpy, awesome, bossy, scared, curious or another I missed.

As you know, our feelings, thinking and behaviour are all connected. We can use our thinking and our behaviour to change how we feel. Each thought you have creates energy within your physical being. The funny thing is we see the world as we are, we look for evidence of what we believe and we attract our beliefs into our world. If you're thinking, 'I'm no good at that,' then you'll look for things in your life that support that thought and then you'll experience low, worrying or anxious energy.

There's no need to beat yourself up, if you've been having pity parties or worry fests. It sucks that the brain can't tell the difference between what's imagined and what's real, if you're not using this real superpower fact to your advantage. Up till now, worry was in charge and wonder was, well, left out in the cold. That firmly stops now. No more creating a lot of what you don't want with your thinking, even lemons, just to prove a point!

The amazing thing is we can rewire our brain because it's so suggestable. If you want a more positive experience to occur then try thinking high-level thoughts like, 'I am lovable,' or 'I am brilliant!' When you think and feel 'I'm enough,' or 'I'm great,' you exude an energy of confidence and in turn attract great experiences into your life. Every thought we have is creating energy, and energy manifests into your experiences. The mind/body connection can literally light up your world. You, my friend, have eyes to see the good and the wisdom to be grateful – you are a veritable genius!

DAY 31: POWERFUL THINKING FOR ME, MYSELF AND I

Recognising how your thoughts negatively affect your life is the first powerful step towards changing your experiences. Remember – you thought about a lemon, felt your mouth water and then your brain believed you were eating a lemon even though you were only visualising one.

Thinking, feeling and believing ...

Write down three areas you want to experience self confidence in:

1. _____

2. _____

3. _____

How would it feel to you in each area if you had more confidence?

1. _____

2. _____

3. _____

Take each area and visualise yourself achieving in it, and then write an affirmation for each area to describe your success – e.g., 'I've got this,' 'I enjoy dancing in public' or 'I am getting better at netball,' 'I feel calm sharing my talent in public' or 'I really love eating more fruit and veg in my diet.'

1. _____

2. _____

3. _____

Know that feeling good with clear intentions for all areas of your life is awesome – this power is the cherry on the already delicious cake!

DAY THIRTY ONE ☀ POWER POINTS TO REMEMBER

Be steady, my manifesting friend – your thoughts can create energy disturbances that momentarily blind you to your greatness, but they can also create dreams that are out of this world. It's not sorcery but it is a little magic as it makes you understand you were born for a purpose, you are here for a reason and you can do great things. The answers are deep inside you, and mindful meditation can help you unleash your inner power to create more acceptance and joy, or even the next big invention to rock the world!

Consider this statement and then finish the following sentence three times.

∞ I BELIEVE IN MYSELF - I CAN DO GREAT THINGS WITH MY LIFE.
I RECOGNISE I AM VALUABLE AND WORTHY ALREADY;
I AM BRILLIANT AND TALENTED. ∞

Three ways I can tap into my inner power and create the reality I want are:

1. _____

2. _____

3. _____

EVERYTHING STARTS WITH ME. I TAP INTO MY INNER POWER AND CREATE THE REALITY I WANT!

Day 31 affirmation

∞ Everything starts with me - I know I can create a brilliant life.
I breathe in power; I breathe out creativity. ∞

😊 Superpower Song for day 31:

🎧 'Life is a Rollercoaster' by Ronan Keating, 🎵
from the album *Ronan*

Day 32

How Can I Be More Resilient?

It might be fun to ask a friend to do this exercise with you – one of your mates who knows you quite well. Of course, you can give it a go by yourself, but remember the old saying – a problem shared is a problem halved – and, anyway, it's good to get help. While you and I might struggle with one thing, a friend may have a great solution. Remember to question: 'Is it true?'

Be your own life coach ...

How can resilience make you feel healthier? Maybe by not worrying over past mistakes, letting things go, accepting we don't always get things right the first time or realising that if we are hurt that hurt does not define us.

How can I feel more resilient?

_____

_____

The great minds of the planet have shown that students with good resilience perform better at school, feel more successful, and have a greater sense of love and kindness towards themselves and others. Going with the flow and being flexible helps build resilience.

How can I be more flexible?

_____

_____

If I was more resilient and flexible, I'd try _____

_____

_____

I have wanted to do that for ages. Go on – give it a go. You can do it.

My brave choice is to (write your goal down in bold letters):

_____

_____

I will achieve my goal.

You've got this!

When will you start? Avoid negative self-chatter which could hold you back. Clear your head of the little voice that says, 'I can't do it,' or 'I don't want to do it,' or 'What if I fail?' Do the magic 3 and put a start date down now.

The big day is:

_____

_____

DAY THIRTY TWO ☀ POWER POINTS TO REMEMBER

I love it when we awaken to the truth that we can replace unhelpful thoughts with helpful ones. It's brilliant because we just naturally stop comparing our growth and our life with others'. We own our thinking and make choices that uplift and inspire us. We also start to feel lighter and happier. People notice when you're easy-going and comfortable in your own skin. It's funny, but the more relaxed you are the more charmed your life is, and rockets of joy just seem to fire your way.

BE YOUR OWN

I CREATE IT IN MY MIND, AND IT
HAPPENS IN MY WORLD

Consider this statement and then finish the following sentence three times.

∞ WHEN IT COMES TO MY GOALS AND DREAMS, I DON'T EXPECT THINGS TO HAPPEN LIKE YESTERDAY. I AM PATIENT AND I TAKE SMALL STEPS (LOTS OF PRACTICE) TOWARDS MY GOALS EACH DAY. I TRUST IN MYSELF; I BELIEVE IT SO I CAN ACHIEVE IT. ∞

Three areas where I could achieve more if I believed more are:

1. _____

2. _____

3. _____

Day 32 affirmation

∞ I am unstoppable - I create with joy and ease. I believe I can achieve.
I breathe in confidence; I breathe out freedom. ∞

😊 Superpower Song for day 32:

🎧 'I've Got the Power' by Karen Drucker, J. D. Martin and David Roth, ♪
from the album *All About Love*

Day 33

Be Open to Change

Listen, change comes whether we like it or not. We've all been pretty low at times in the confidence or resilience department when facing change. The thing is that because it is constant we have to learn to be playful with it and not take it too seriously. Learning to ride the waves of change is what resilience is all about. By learning to explore what presents itself, we ride the waves of change. In the training world we use an easy acronym which can be helpful:

C – Choose your response, and take one deep breath.

H – Have awareness of the mind/body connection.

A – Accept 'what is' and respond to yourself kindly.

N – Notice you can care for yourself with your thoughts.

G – Give yourself time to adjust. Be gentle.

E – Encourage your thoughts to be loving and kind.

The world can be a big and confusing space, that's for sure, and the world of our emotions is no different. It is like the ocean: sometimes flat, serene and calm, and sometimes wild with crashing surf or inviting with small, rocking waves.

The weather directs the mood of the ocean – be it high winds or still sunny days, the water responds. For us a storm might be brewing with friends and family or stress at school, and like the ocean we chop and change. One minute we are relaxed or happy and the next edgy or irritated. Whether we are floating along on a happy wave or swept away with anger, we tend to experience small (and sometimes big) emotional ups and downs each day.

What we are doing here is learning to harness our emotions. We can learn how to float with our feelings, letting them wash over us, or how to surf the big feelings, not letting them crash over us. You are the manifestation master, and by taking control you get to know how to ride the waves, and you develop the CHANGE skills to surf any breaker that comes your way. Let's do this!

DAY 33: SURFING THE WAVES

OK, let's be with what is. Observe your feelings – just notice how you are feeling right now. As a feeling arises, become the witness of it. Find yourself watching it with kind eyes.

Let yourself feel what you are feeling – experience your feeling as a wave coming and going. Try not to block the feeling, don't try to get rid of it and don't try to push it away or hold on to it. Just be with it. Our pleasant, neutral and unpleasant feelings are part of us and natural to have.

Don't try to make the feeling bigger or smaller, just be with what is. Now remember, you are not the feeling and you don't need to act on it – you can choose a different response.

Feelings are just feelings and they are part of us all, but they don't define us unless we act on them. You can use the mind/body connection to your advantage and be still with your feelings; getting used to being more comfortable with your feelings helps you.

Don't judge your feelings. Remember, mindfulness is moment-by-moment non-judgmental awareness with love and kindness.

You are on the hero's journey: you can accept all of you, you know you are human and you have an ocean of emotion. But remember, each emotion is just a drop of water in a vast ocean of experience and sometimes you'll ride waves of happiness and success and other times challenges and hurt. They are all part of you and they all deserve your kindness.

In time you'll welcome all of your emotions equally and become comfortable being with what is. Remember – to struggle with reality is a waste of energy, but to accept what is and take action that supports you, even if that means feeling the fear and doing it anyway, is the stuff of heroes.

This might sound crazy, but the trick to becoming a true hero with true power is to accept your fears. Keep them close, hug them as part of you, bathe them in a bomb of compassion – because if you avoid your fears you give them power. It's funny, but when you sit with fear and just let it arise it can fizzle out. Our fears are part of us, and if we don't accept ourselves who else can? Maybe your fear is a guide to who you truly are. Maybe it is the opportunity to take your courage and show up.

Consider this statement and then finish the following sentence three times.

∞ I FEEL THE FEAR AND DO IT ANYWAY. WITH COURAGE
I ACCEPT MYSELF AND SHOW MY FEARS SELF-COMPASSION.
I GAIN UNDERSTANDING OF MYSELF WHEN I ACCEPT MYSELF. ∞

Three areas of my life where I could accept my fears are:

1. _____

2. _____

3. _____

Sometimes even when it is scary you just have to rise to the challenge – your greatness depends on it!

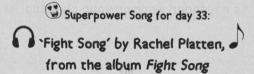

Day 33 affirmation

∞ I accept I am enough. I breathe in courage; I breathe
out confidence. I am enough just as I am. ∞

😊 Superpower Song for day 33:
🎧 'Fight Song' by Rachel Platten, ♪
from the album *Fight Song*

Day 34

Freedom Right Where You Are

EXPLORING PLEASANT, UNPLEASANT AND NEUTRAL SENSATIONS

LIFE IS LIKE A BOX OF CHOCOLATES

'Life is like a box of chocolates – you never know what you're gonna get,' Forrest Gump shares in the movie. This is a good reminder to embrace change and face our fears, and recognise that some of those chocolates we will like and others we won't, and then there will be those we are indifferent about. As a wonder warrior your challenge is to accept whatever chocolate may be offered to you from time to time. Your chocolates might be people, events, feelings or thoughts and you won't love them all, but you can't pretend they don't exist. We are all pretty resistant to change, yet underneath this resistance can live incredible value – when we take the time to receive these 'chocolates' with openness and courage, we grow in resilience.

Think of an event in school or at home where you were resistant to change. Notice how your thoughts created sensations in your body, the majority probably being unpleasant. With hindsight and acceptance of what is or surrender to the change, how might you approach the change differently?

POWER Tip

Remember **this too shall pass**, when the next wave of change you find challenging presents itself.

Thinking of life like a box of chocolates reminds us to be present for all of the thoughts and feelings we have. We can't deny them or pretend they are not there. My mum loves the coffee chocolate, but I think it's gross. Just because I don't like it as much as other chocolates doesn't mean it won't be in the box!

The Vietnamese monk, poet and peace activist Thich Nhat Hanh invites us to care for our anger or dark emotion as if it were a small child, or a friend in pain, sharing, 'Sit down with it, be compassionate towards it, make it tea. In this way, it can heal.'

The key here is that the painful or troubling parts of ourselves should be welcomed and cared for with kindness, not suppressed or buried in layers of shame, guilt or fear. The way we treat ourselves is the way we treat others. If we are gentle with ourselves, we will be gentle with others.

Consider this statement and then finish the following sentence three times.

∞ I LOVE AND ACCEPT MY UNCOMFORTABLE THOUGHTS - THEY
ARE PART OF ME JUST AS MY JOY IS, AND I ACCEPT ALL OF ME.
ALL MY EXPERIENCE DESERVES MY KINDNESS. ∞

Three uncomfortable shadow thoughts I don't accept in me are:

1. _____

2. _____

3. _____

I am loving and kind with my thinking –
it transforms my life!

Day 34 affirmation

∞ I accept all of my experience: pleasant, unpleasant and neutral.
I breathe in kindness; I breathe out acceptance. ∞

😺 Superpower Song for day 34:

🎧 'You Are a Star' by Fischy Music, 🎵
from the album *Build Up*

Day 35

Easy as A, B, C, D

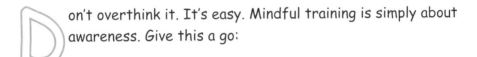

Don't overthink it. It's easy. Mindful training is simply about awareness. Give this a go:

1. Anatomy – taking note of our body. Sit comfortably with a straight back, hands resting lightly on your knees and your eyes shut.

2. Breathing – belly breathing. This breathing becomes the focus of mindful practice, producing a rhythmic flow of in and out breaths.

3. Counting – breathing is practised in sets of ten. Each in/out breath is counted as one – continuing up to ten. When you reach ten, start again at one and repeat the count to ten.

4. Distractions – initially it is almost impossible to continue breathing/counting to ten without your mind wandering or being distracted by internal or external musings. Each time you catch yourself in a distraction, acknowledge it, let it go, then bring your attention back to your breathing and commence counting from one to ten again.

Repeat this for anywhere between two and ten minutes, a couple of times a day. The more the better, but five minutes twice a day will produce immediate and spectacular results.

Each time we do this we are **flexing our brain focus muscle** and forming a new neural pathway. As our attention muscle gets stronger (and it will!) we get the positive benefits of increased focus and attentional power in our everyday lives. This has a cumulative effect of improving our quality of life, happiness and well-being.

DAY 35: JUST STOP

Just a second gives you a choice ... Let's choose to make life really simple today. Apply the STOP theory to any challenges that come your way today:

Stop what you are doing

Take a few deep breaths

Observe your mind/emotions

Proceed with choice – e.g., responding not reacting

DAY THIRTY FIVE ☀ POWER POINTS TO REMEMBER

We all need time just to be. It is good to take time out from solving the world's or our own problems. We need to empty ourselves of all the thoughts and emotions that keep us busy, and simply be. As we breathe in the present moment, we increase our clarity and simplify our life. We give ourselves a holiday for the mind and just press pause on the movie screen of our busy life for a short time. This feels really peaceful and we can just exhale.

Consider this statement and then finish the following sentence three times.

∞ I CAN SIMPLIFY MY LIFE WHEN I BECOME STILL AND REST
IN THE PRESENT MOMENT. I STOP BEING A HUMAN DOING
AND START BEING A HUMAN BEING, AND I FEEL FREE. ∞

Three areas where being present and still will help me with improved decision-making are:

1. _____

2. _____

3. _____

I empty my mind and I am filled with clarity and vision. It is good to just be in the present moment.

WEEK SIX

THE NEW WAY OF BEING, SEEING AND LIVING

STILL IN ACT THREE

- ✔ Resurrection
- ✔ Return with elixir

ACT THREE, WEEK SIX – THE ROAD BACK FOR HARRY

The weeks absolutely flew by and the qualifiers' rounds were happening for the county running club this week – it was a big deal for Harry.

'Hiya love, I've just made you a super green smoothie minus the kale,' smiled Harry's mum. 'My job is to fuel fantastic, fast – er – furlongs,' she said, her face crumpling into laughter.

'I'm not a horse, mum!' He laughed too.

'I know, but I couldn't think of another word beginning with "f" that was active!' she said, still smiling. 'I'm so proud of you, Harry, standing up to Charlie [aka Snake, to us] – it'll be great to have this business behind you once and for all. Come here give us a hug, love.'

'Life does feel good,' he thought, then mid-hug they heard a booming RAT A TAT TAT knock at the door. 'Jeez, where's the fire?' thought Harry.

Ruby opened the door and Tom burst into the hall, blurting out breathlessly, 'You and Snake are head to head in the qualifiers for the county times. Can you believe it, mate? What are we going to do?' he asked, shaking his head in disbelief.

'Get down there and make the times. I want this for me and the team,' said Harry triumphantly, moving towards the front door. 'Let's go,' he said assertively. His heart was pounding slightly, but he was determined to stick with his power mindset.

Ruby grabbed him in another bear hug. 'Good luck, love. Be careful. You've got this – I know you have, I am sure of it!'

Harry smiled, thinking, 'Who's she trying to convince, me or her?'

The tension was palpable at the track – everyone was psyched, waiting to be called for their race. Harry was breathing deeply, ready and set to face the challenge. 'Race first, deal with Snake after.' His thoughts were interrupted by the tannoy calling his race. He gritted his teeth and simply said to himself, 'Breathe, Harry. You've got this. You can do it,' as he walked to the start line.

He knelt down, mentally saying, 'I will have the perfect start.' Totally in the zone, he didn't even glance in Snake's direction. The gun went off for the 200 metres sprint …

Harry was passing the finish line, not sure how he'd got there. He looked up at the times, and – **boom** – he'd won! The crowds were roaring applause – he felt fantastic as he hit the floor and lay panting to get his breath back.

His team mates pulled him up, clapping and cheering him. He'd actually beaten the fastest county record by 0.75 of a second. 'Result!' they were all shouting and cheering.

Flying high and feeling strong, Harry knew it was time to end this nonsense with Charlie. He felt empowered and happy as he walked over to Charlie, putting his hand out and saying, 'Great race. We both beat the county record. On fire, Charlie, you shaved 0.33 off it.'

Charlie looked at him, with mixed emotions crossing his face. 'Yeah. Great race but not the end of all our battles, Harry,' he said.

'Really? You're going to go there?' said Harry incredulously.

'Yeah, I am. We're not done,' sneered Charlie.

'We are, because I'm not scared of you, mate. You don't worry me anymore. Your choice: we can either work together on the team to smash new records or you can just stay out of my way,' said Harry, walking away with a powerful inner smile.

Paula thinks:

Harry has entered his new world of confidence and resilience; he is demonstrating his power mindset by being clear on what he wants. He has put all of his mental and physical training into action and he is reaping the rewards. He is feeling his old self, more in control of his destiny, and he is not prepared to be pushed around by anyone.

He is owning the fact that anything is possible, and he is not limiting himself anymore with worrying thoughts about the past. He's decided he won't be defined by his past experience with Snake or anyone else, including his own demons – the dragon thoughts of fear and anxiety.

He won't run on FEAR (False Evidence Appearing Real) any longer. He is changing his attitude and his future. Where he didn't trust he had the power in the past, he now knows he does and is taking action to prove it.

Harry is doing amazingly and all of his practice over the last few weeks is really paying off. Training the brain and the body takes discipline and practice. Do you remember we said at the beginning that greatness is grown and if we practise we can achieve almost anything? Well, Harry is amazing proof that this is true and he has certainly grown in greatness.

He's even feeling the kindness bug and has stopped calling Charlie 'Snake'. This shows Harry can be the bigger person – he's not entertaining a feud or being bullied. He points the way to connection and compassion, suggesting they train together on a shared goal. Harry is leading by example and generously sharing his **I've Got the Power** kind-natured spirit.

Go Harry – own that power!

ACT THREE, WEEK SIX – THE ROAD BACK FOR OLIVIA

'What's the matter? Is everything alright?' said Pops, looking alarmed.

'I'm confused, Pops. I didn't want mum to die. I wish I could've saved her. I want her to be there watching me next week, with you and dad ...' said Olivia, with pulse-pounding anxiety and tears washing over her face.

'Oh darling, it is so very sad. Your mum would be so proud of you and her love is always with you, like a guardian angel watching over you,' said Pops, drawing Olivia close into a hug.

'Mum was my biggest fan – she always made me feel amazing and special about my dancing. We had such fun together, Pops, I miss her!' She paused.

'My heart feels broken, Pops. Last week after the *Strictly* show I was so happy, and then guilty straight afterwards. I don't know how to feel, I miss mum so much. I just want things to be normal.' She cried.

'Grief is like the ocean,' said Pops. 'It ebbs and flows. One day you are OK. The next day you are not. It's going to take time, love.'

'I don't like people singling me out or feeling sorry for me. That's a big part of me not wanting to open the show, Pops.'

'I see. I know I've asked you before about going to the support group – it might be good to talk about your mum, with others who are also bereaved. It's good to get help to know you're not alone,' he said, his eyes glistening with tears.

'I feel ready now, Pops. I think it will help, and that girl I spoke to on the buddy line the first time said you also get the chance to help others by sharing your own story. And she said it's like we don't feel so alone, like you're not the only one.'

'The love you share with your mum, darling, will never go – she's always in your heart.'

'I know, but I want to hold her and for her to hold me,' said Olivia, with a melancholy look of love and sadness in her eyes. Then she felt a wash of love fill her heart and embrace her in such comfort, just like her mum used to. She felt safe, secure, loved and protected by her mum, her angel, as Pops had said.

Paula thinks:

Olivia is really owning the power mindset, growing in self-acceptance and learning she needs to feel her pain to heal her pain. She knows her hurt is deep and she is ready to ask for help. She's feeling strong enough to deal with the deep loneliness and grief of her mum's death. She is really being mindful and compassionate with herself.

She realises she doesn't want to be in the spotlight or singled out because of her grief, and that is spilling over into her worries around standing out – like opening the show at the school Strictly competition. This insight will help her deal with her anxiety around the show. She is also accepting that her dancing is part of her unique talents.

Olivia is ditching the worry mindset here as she has stopped fighting with reality. She is accepting her deep pain and she is also learning not to obsess over tomorrow, being more present to what she is thinking and feeling right now. She is beginning to believe anything is possible, including her feeling OK again.

She just wants everything to be normal, but now she's realising that her 'normal' means it's time for help from others who share the same normal experience. She recognises this connection and the fact that we are all connected will help her move through the grieving process. She won't run on FEAR (False Evidence Appearing Real) any longer. She recognises she is not alone.

She is also connecting to all the feelings of love she has for her mum as a source of strength and loving care – now the thought of her mum, as her angel, will help her transform the deep grief and pain she feels and connect to the wonderful source and power of love her mum is in her life.

The most important point is that Olivia is accepting her feelings are normal and to be expected when such tragedy hits your life. Olivia is growing her self-compassion and resilience as she behaves in ways that prove she is loving to herself. She recognises we are all connected and sees she doesn't have to do everything by herself– she can ask for help and support, and she does, another great act of self-love.

Day 36

An Attitude of Gratitude

WHAT IS GRATITUDE?

Gratitude is uplifting and inspiring, such a positive feeling. Listen – we get so busy we forget to focus on what's good in our lives, and take what we have for granted. I love gratitude because it reminds us we already have lots of reasons to be cheerful. Like having a place to live, food, clean water, friends, family and our health. We can see, walk, talk, laugh, dance and play – we have so much choice. Like other positive emotions, feeling grateful on a regular basis can have a big effect on our lives. Check these benefits out! What's not to like or be grateful for?

Physical:

⭐ Having a stronger immune system

⭐ Being less bothered by aches and pains

⭐ Having lower blood pressure

⭐ Exercising more and taking better care of your health

⭐ Sleeping longer and feeling more refreshed upon waking.

Psychological:

⭐ Feeling higher levels of positive emotions

⭐ Feeling more alert, alive and awake

⭐ Feeling more joy and pleasure

⭐ Feeling more optimism and happiness.

Social:

⭐ Feeling more helpful, generous, and compassionate

⭐ Feeling more forgiving

⭐ Being more outgoing

⭐ Feeling less lonely and isolated.

You've got it – the best brain researchers across the planet tell us if you have an 'attitude of gratitude' you will experience all of the above advantages, and more.

DAY 36: GRATITUDE GIVES – PAY IT FORWARD

What if you were born to save the world with one small act of kindness at a time? What would your hero schedule look like? If you had to don the superpower cape of kindness and cross the dimension of indifference to making a difference, purging yourself of apathy, how would you practise? Here are a few ideas to pop in your weekly training plan.

This week the world needs more love by:

💜 Exercising gratitude muscles – every morning write a gratitude journal (remember the simple things: family, health, food, friends, etc.)

💜 Making an effort to deliver a random act of kindness

💜 Giving a little love – it all comes back to you … think of three ways to do this

💜 Saying 'thank you' more often, and writing thank-you notes

💜 Setting yourself a daily hug target – feel the oxytocin grow!

💜 Connecting with others – text your loved ones a message of thanks

💜 Practising mindfulness to appreciate each moment

💜 Listing five things you have to be grateful for

💜 Practising some positive thinking by acknowledging one ungrateful thought per day and then replacing it with a grateful one

💜 Posting words, photos and objects of gratitude in your home – remember, the brain likes the familiar, so let's make kindness more familiar.

I quite like the idea of us shining our inner light of gratitude – it just makes everything seem so much better. We know by now that everything starts and ends with us, so we might as well create more of what we want in our life. The thing is that what we focus on we get, so focusing on gratitude gives us more things to be grateful for. Switching on the light of gratitude in our minds is the road to health and happiness.

I am grateful for...
Sun   Health   our   Memories
Mother   earth
Passion   emotion   Food
Music   love   smile
emotion   Soul   Joy

WHEN I AM MINDFUL I SEE SO MANY THINGS I AM GRATEFUL FOR

Consider this statement and then finish the following sentence three times.

∞ I LOVE GRATITUDE, IT IS AN ANTIDOTE TO STRESS.
I SWITCH ON THE LIGHT OF GRATITUDE AND IT FEELS GREAT -
I LOVE SO MANY THINGS IN MY LIFE ALREADY. ∞

Three areas where I already have reasons to be cheerful are:

1. _____

2. _____

3. _____

Day 37

Gratitude and Kindness

Catch the happiness virus. 'Happy' hormones such as dopamine and serotonin are released when we perform acts of kindness or are grateful for someone or something. Check out these ideas to increase your happy hormones and make the world a better place too.

★ Talk to someone at school who seems a bit alone

★ Post a flower to a friend unexpectedly

★ Write small cards of thanks, appreciating your friends and family

★ Give your little brother or sister a break, let them in your room

★ Smile when you feel frustrated (more calm energy in the universe!)

★ Share lunch with a friend

★ Volunteer in the community – e.g., visit the elderly and brighten their week!

★ Give up your seat on the tube/bus

★ Tell someone they are beautiful, even when they are not feeling down

★ Really listen to someone

⭐ Stop and ask people if they need help when you see they do

⭐ Make extra cakes for friends at school when you are baking

⭐ Share your time or money to support a good cause

⭐ See the creative, imaginative genius in yourself

⭐ Be a buddy to someone who's lonely or in hospital

⭐ Tell people you love that you love them

⭐ Compliment a stranger

⭐ Let people in the canteen go before you in the queue

⭐ If someone is sitting alone, offer to join them.

Feel good by doing good

Being grateful and kind boosts our immune system, it helps us be more resilient and helps us cope with the challenges that happen in our life. Obviously, being kind doesn't mean stressful things won't occur, but it does mean you'll have a better ability to cope. Check out Google – there's loads of proof. The new buzz word on mindfulness and loving kindness is **kindfulness**. The Dalai Lama shares, 'Be kind whenever possible. It is always possible.' Nice to know – let's give it a go.

Consider this statement and then finish the following sentence three times.

∞ I LOVE CREATING MY LIFE WITH KINDFULNESS -
I AM FULL OF UNLIMITED KINDFULNESS.
I AM BUZZING WITH AN ATTITUDE OF GRATITUDE. ∞

Three ways in which I can introduce more kindfulness into my life are:

1. _____

2. _____

3. _____

I shout out for kindfulness - it is a power I tap into easily and effortlessly

Day 37 affirmation

∞ I love shouting out about kindfulness - it makes me feel better and the world a better place. I breathe in kindfulness; I breathe out gratitude. ∞

😊 Superpower Song for day 37:

🎧 'Rule the World' by Take That, ♪
from the album *Beautiful World*

Day 38

Catching Goodness ...

isten, goodness begins with you. Part of being kind to others is making sure we are kind to ourselves. Self-compassion, as we've said, is about being understanding and accepting of ourselves. This self-acceptance and understanding leads to being more understanding and accepting (tolerant) of others and understanding them more too, so it's great for relationships with friends or at home. It helps us develop patience with ourselves as we are moved, hurt or overwhelmed by things happening in our life. Catching compassion feels good and grows your self-esteem – it cultivates a kind heart.

💜 Self-compassion means you understand you're not perfect, you won't be right all the time and sometimes things won't go your way.

💜 Being kind to yourself means you understand that there will be good days and bad days, and on the bad days you don't beat yourself up – you know it's all just part of being human. Sure, you can review the day and gain insight on small changes you can make to improve the day, always in the knowledge that the day does not define you.

💜 Goodness means you know you're enough no matter what happens. The good heart in you knows you are enough just as you are, mistakes and all.

💜 A good heart is a safe haven when you feel overwhelmed – you can anchor yourself in the knowledge that you are not your mistakes or your triumphs. You value your experiences and see them as opportunities to learn and grow.

💜 Self-compassion, kindness and a good heart replace worry with wonder. They embrace inner critical dialogue with little bombs of love – e.g., 'I resolve to only speak to myself with kindness, the way my best friend would,' or 'I am going to concentrate on all the things I get right or can be grateful for.' These choices will help you feel calmer, which feels better – you can pause unsupportive thoughts, the choice is yours.

Isn't it brilliant that we can get a sense of freedom from recognising it's okay to be where we are right now? You can choose to learn and grow, for sure, but you are also lucky to be one of a kind. Yes, you are different to everyone else, and that is great. All successful heroes know worrying about differences and not leading with your A game constantly does not make us flawed – it just makes us human. Be kind to yourself whenever possible, and it's always possible!

ONE OF A KIND

I BACK MYSELF AND LOVE THAT I AM ONE OF A KIND!

Consider this statement and then finish the following sentence three times.

∞ I LOVE THAT I AM ONE OF A KIND. I AM UNIQUE AND HAVE UNLIMITED POTENTIAL TO LOVE AND BE LOVED. I HAVE BUCKETS OF SELF-COMPASSION; I BACK MYSELF. ∞

Three ways I can be more kind to myself and back myself are:

1. _____

2. _____

3. _____

Day 38 affirmation

∞ I am one of a kind and love it. I breathe in curiosity; I breathe out compassion. ∞

😊 Superpower Song for day 38:

🎧 'Over the Rainbow' by Israel Kamakawiwo'ole, ♪ from the album Ka 'Ano'i

Day 39

Loving Kindness Is Power

Loving-kindness meditation is a brilliant practice to boost your well-being. It is the practice of directing positive thoughts and well wishes to ourselves and others. Start by doing the magic 3.

Continue sitting comfortably with your eyes closed, and imagine what you wish for in your life. The four phrases that you either say out loud or think silently during the practice are:

May I/you be safe

May I/you be healthy and strong

May I/you be happy

May I/you be peaceful and at ease

You repeat these wishes, directing them first to yourself and then towards different people in your life, as follows:

1. Start by directing the phrases to yourself.

2. Next, direct the kindfulness towards someone you feel thankful for or who has helped you.

3. Now visualise someone you feel neutral about – someone you neither like nor dislike. Direct the thoughts to that person.

4. Next, direct the thoughts to someone you don't like or who you are having a difficult time dealing with.

5. Finally, direct the kindfulness towards everyone universally: *may all beings everywhere be happy.*

DAY THIRTY NINE ☀ POWER POINTS TO REMEMBER

What's amazing about the loving-kindness meditation is that we are encouraged to generate feelings of kindness, love and friendliness. Yet, again, the bottom line is – it is good for us. Don't take my word for it – the research shows this practice produces physical changes in the brain causing the empathy and compassion regions of the brain to grow. This is awesome: if your brain actually grows when you practise then it stands to reason, as we've said all along, whatever you practise, each time you do it, it gets easier!

Consider this statement and then finish the following sentence three times.

I AM THE BOSS OF MY BRAIN - I CREATE GREATNESS WITH MY MIND!

∞ I LOVE CREATING MY WONDER MINDSET - THROUGH ALL MY PRACTICES I AM CREATING (NEURO) PATHWAYS TO GREATNESS. MY CONTINUOUS EFFORT PAYS OFF. ∞

Three areas where I can put more effort in to grow a brain of greatness are:

1. _____

2. _____

3. _____

Day 39 affirmation

∞ I create greatness with my mind - the more I practise the stronger connections I create. I create feelings of well-being. I breathe in well-being; I breathe out greatness. ∞

😊 Superpower Song for day 39:

🎧 'Good Feeling' by Flo Rida, ♪
from the album *Wild Ones*

Day 40

Big Brother's Five Ways to Well-Being

The Mental Health Foundation's five ways to well-being are:

I love Emma Watson's quote: 'If we stop defining each other by what we are not and starting defining ourselves by what we are, we can all be free.' 'Hang on a minute,' I hear you cry. 'What's that got to do with the five ways to well-being?' A lot, actually, you see, when we feel free, we can show up more authentically in all of these areas. The authentic us is the best version of ourselves we can share with the world. Let's think about the five ways a bit more and how we can rock them in the world.

Give – your time, your words, your presence

Be active – do what you can, enjoy what you do, move your mood

Keep learning – embrace new experiences, see opportunities, surprise yourself!

Connect – talk, listen, be there, feel connected

Take notice – remember the simple things that give you joy

Authenticity just means being true to ourselves, it means we don't feel the need to hide our true nature, we're comfortable in our skin and we can shine more in our actions, words and ideas. We move from 'not sure of myself' to 'look out world, here I come!' Wouldn't you rather show up with more passion for what you are doing? It's only going to make the five ways to well-being more fantastic, fascinating and fun as you practise them.

DAY FORTY ☀ POWER POINTS TO REMEMBER

OK, so let's remind ourselves what 'manifestation' means: in the main, it is the ability to attract, create and turn any vision into reality. Thinking of the five ways to well-being and being true to our authentic self, practising them authentically means you will be creating the world of your dreams and possibly become the happiest person you know. From a life of woe to one of woah is the way to go. You can apply the five ways to attract and create more confidence in your life, try out new hobbies, make friends and, well, really, just about anything.

Consider this statement and then finish the following sentence three times.

∞ I HAVE THE POWER TO ATTRACT AND CREATE MY DREAMS.
MY LIFE IS FULL OF UNLIMITED POTENTIAL. I APPRECIATE THE
SMALL THINGS IN LIFE AND KNOW THEY ARE ALREADY PART
OF MY WELL-BEING. I CREATE HAPPINESS AND JOY. ∞

Three areas where I can attract and create more joy and happiness in my life are:

1. _____

2. _____

3. _____

I GET THE SECRET TO HAPPINESS IS APPRECIATING THE SMALL THINGS I ATTRACT AND CREATE WITH A KIND HEART AND MIND!

Day 40 affirmation

∞ When I love my brain my brain loves me. I breathe in self-love;
I breathe out happiness. ∞

😊 Superpower Song for day 40:
🎧 'We Are the Champions' by Queen, ♪
from the album *News of the World*

Day 41

Let's Get the Hug Bug

You really deserve a hug for getting this far – it hasn't been easy, for sure, but it feels brilliant, right? Can you hear the crowds cheering your name – lots of plaudits, pats on the back, celebrations and huge hugs for taking this adventure and getting out there and being great?

We couldn't leave without a chat about how awesome hugs are for our well-being. You've got it – the greatest scientists across the planet have found hugs create the kindness hormone oxytocin, also known as

the hug-bug or cuddle chemical. In a nutshell, hugging feels great and creates happy hormones.

Today I want you to charge up your happy hormones by taking the hug challenge.

Stepping truly out of the shadow of worry, fire up the hug bug and let's feel wonderful. Success is guaranteed – you've got this, you are unstoppable and **you've got the power**, so let's go for it. 'What do I need to do?' you ask, bursting with excitement (well, maybe not bursting!).

Simple – you just need to activate the cuddle chemical by hugging at least seven people or pets for at least seven days and feel free, fantastic and brilliant in the process. Go on, give it a go. There's no time like the present to get started.

It turns out that transforming our life from worry to wonder feels great in the main. I mean, come on, you must be smiling after just hugging someone, right? Isn't it great how having a power mindset makes life so much better? You've proved to yourself that whatever you want to be good at you can be by changing the way you think. You also know the way you think attracts and brings your dreams into reality. What's not to like? I'm so glad you took the risk and accepted our *You've Got the Power* adventure – to change your world with your thoughts, speech and actions. Go you!

Consider this statement and then finish the following sentence three times.

∞ I'VE GOT THE POWER - I CREATE MY LIFE JUST HOW I WANT IT TO BE. I LOVE WHO I AM - I'M NOT WAITING FOR ANYONE ELSE TO TELL ME I AM GOOD ENOUGH, I KNOW I AM. I AM POWERFUL - I CAN AND WILL DO GREAT THINGS, INCLUDING GETTING THE HUG BUG! ∞

Three ways I can change the world one hug at time for the better are:

1. _____

2. _____

3. _____

Day 41 affirmation

∞ Hugging to celebrate or commiserate is kind to do - it makes me feel great. I breathe in kindness; I breathe out happiness. ∞

😎 Superpower Song for day 41:

🎧 Good Vibrations' by The Beach Boys, ♪ from the album *Good Vibrations*

Day 42

The Meaning of Life

Remember in the introduction we noted the *Hitchhiker's Guide to the Galaxy* says number 42 is the answer to life, the universe and everything? So, here we are in our journey at number 42 – the Holy Grail of our adventure. What do you think? We may not have all the answers, but we definitely know we have a say in our happiness by how we think, act and speak. We know we are magical creators and we have the ability to create the life of our dreams, so that's pretty awesome.

You've got the power – you have the secrets to a happier life and now, like any great inventor, you'll need to keep experimenting with what works best for you. The key is you keep practising with curiosity, wonder and imagination to unlock the life of your dreams. Remember – you are made for greatness and your life truly matters. Only you can make your particular difference in the world, so make sure you do.

If you only make one difference a day, make that difference with a kind heart. Over the last six weeks you've learnt loads of ways to do that. You've got this. Good luck!

Here's to you living the good life!

THE HAPPY-HORMONE MEDITATION

♥ Become aware of your body and your posture, and gently focus on your breath. Now remember all the things you have to be happy for and all the kind acts you have done. Simply breathe into the lovely feelings of happiness these memories create.

♥ Really associate with the time you are thinking about: turn up the brightness on the image you have, strengthen the sensations of gratitude and happiness you are experiencing in your physical body or listen for the joy and laughter you may be hearing.

♥ Now bring your attention back to your breath, and gently draw the breath into your heart. Imagine it is warm, like glorious golden sunshine, and on the out-breath let that light flood your whole being with warm, cosy feelings of gratitude and kindness.

♥ Your heart becomes like a mini sun within your chest, shining a flood of warmth and happiness throughout your body with every out-breath.

DAY FORTY TWO ☀ POWER POINTS TO REMEMBER

Wow! Day 42 – we have made it. Your greatness is an inside job, remember this. Do the practices and follow the strategies to sustain your hero-like sense of confidence and happiness. That's all you've got to do – **practice**.

Consider this statement and then finish the following sentence three times.

∞ I HAVE THE POWER TO ATTRACT AND CREATE MY DREAMS. MY LIFE IS FULL OF UNLIMITED POTENTIAL. I APPRECIATE THE SMALL THINGS IN LIFE AND KNOW THEY ARE ALREADY PART OF MY WELL-BEING. I CREATE HAPPINESS AND JOY. ∞

Three areas where I can attract and create more joy and happiness in my life are:

1. _____

2. _____

3. _____

I get the secret to happiness is appreciating
the small things – I attract and create
with a kind heart and mind!

Day 42 affirmation

∞ When I love my mind, my mind loves me. I breathe in self-love;
I breathe out happiness. ∞

😺 Superpower Song for day 42:

🎧 'Simply the Best' by Tina Turner, from the album *Foreign Affair* ♪

😺 Week 6 inspiration:

'The Hero's Journey according to Joseph Campbell', video by
Matthew Winkler and Kirill Yeretsky, published on YouTube by
Ueber-Brands –https://youtu.be/d1Zxt28ff-E

HERO HARRY'S NEW BRILLIANT BIO

Week six – return with the elixir

Harry was feeling amazing – everything was changing for the better. It seemed Charlie had taken him at his word, as everything was cool on that front. The power mantras had really helped rewire his brain – so 42 might just be the meaning of life, the universe and everything!

'Hey, Tom, it's weird how I let Charlie get to me for so long,' said Harry.

'I know, mate, what he was saying wasn't true – he was just trying to make himself feel more powerful,' Tom said, thoughtfully. 'Truth be known, mate, he's probably more insecure and vulnerable than most of us or he wouldn't do it.'

'Yeah, you're right. Let's get warmed up for the races,' said Harry.

He looked up into the stalls and saw his mum frantically waving and his dad shrugging his shoulders with a knowing smirk. They had often teased his mum over how excited she got at events, and he was happy that they were there together to watch him. He'd definitely moved on from worry to wonder in this department, and knew that, whatever happened, they loved him.

Harry had really upped his game – he was prepped and feeling fantastic in life. You've guessed it – the crowds went crazy, clapping and cheering and, of course, Harry won the race.

He stood, smiling – his world would never be the same again. Everything was familiar, yet it had all changed because he'd changed his thinking. He really felt he had the power. As he glanced across the field, he could see a kid in a Yoda mask. He laughed to himself, imagining his mum, when he told her, saying, 'Love, it's a sign from the universe – the force is with you!' He knew her well, because that's exactly what she did say …

Paula thinks:

This is the final stage of your hero's journey, and Harry has changed in miraculous ways and is putting his superpowers to the test. It's brilliant that he won the race, but what's even better is he's been implementing what he's learnt over the last 42 days as changes in his daily life.

He's used the lessons to heal the wounds of his old thinking and shown up as a Jedi in his own life. He's transformed his challenges with Charlie and gained confidence from his success in running. Successful change in one area of his life, running, gave him the courage to change in other areas, like standing up to Charlie.

He has come to terms with his parents' divorce and is feeling happier and more confident back in his ordinary world after his adventure. These are just three great, obvious changes but there will be many more, less obvious ones, like feeling more relaxed and connected, being clear on what he wants and knowing he has the power.

He returns with the elixir of a new mindset. His new beginnings include old wounds being resolved with Charlie, and great new connections through the running club. Another great thing here is that through doing something he loves and standing up to his fears he has naturally gained more contentment and acceptance around his parents' divorce.

It just goes to show how growing as a person from worry to wonder makes life better all round – the butterfly effect shows up beautifully here in Harry's life.

Well done, Harry, we love you – you are a stand-out hero and have achieved off-the-scale personal awesomeness. Yay you!

OLIVIA'S CELEBRATION STORY

Livy and Katie took to the dance floor as the dramatic pasodoble music blared out, sparking a sense of drama fit for the expected intensity of the performance. Livy was taking the male role, so her story-telling was vital to the performance. She was playing the matador and Katie was playing the bull ...

Earlier, they had been waiting backstage anxiously. Katie was looking lovely and not garish, in loads of make-up and fake tan, dressed in Lycra with a feather boa around her neck. She squealed, 'OMG, I have a great idea! Because I'm the bull in this performance, you can see me as the dragon of worry you need to slay, to help you. What do you think? It's genius, isn't it? Well?' she asked triumphantly.

Livy laughed, straightening her bolero jacket, and with a dramatic flounce of her cape said, 'You're on.' She didn't let on that she had already decided, with the help of Pops, that was exactly what she was going to do.

Wow – the story-telling was amazing and they both played their roles brilliantly, giving an amazing performance, receiving a stonking maximum 40 points from the judges. Woo woo!

As they came off stage, Livy's dad was standing in the wings, holding a gorgeous golden puppy. Smiling, he said, 'You smashed it – well done – and Toto thinks so too! I know you and mum always wanted a dog, so I thought, what a great surprise.'

'Oh dad, I'm so happy I could cry,' she said, hugging him and Toto, tears of happiness and relief glistening in her eyes.

Paula thinks:

Something really magical happens when we commit to ourselves, and Olivia is beginning to trust in this magic again. She's had a tough time and she is emerging back into her life with fresh insights on living and loving.

It was a great idea, too, to use the pasodoble as a metaphor for Livy to face her demons of being afraid of standing out. The dance is based around the concept of the matador facing a bull in the bullring. She really owned her power and turned her fear into excitement to add to her performance. Remember – words and feelings only have the meaning we give them.

No major external shifts have happened, but Olivia is seeing her world differently because of her inner change work of self-care and self-acceptance. She is learning to be with her grief, feel safe and enjoy life again. As she trusts herself once more, she can also trust in the world more.

Toto will bring great joy to her heart. It is a known fact that the companionship of animals to play, stroke, walk and have fun with brings increased love, and of course that will continue to support Olivia's healing and acceptance of her mum's passing.

Gaining confidence and a sense of achievement from her dancing gave Olivia the courage to be vulnerable and ask for help. She has stopped fighting her feelings of vulnerability and learnt that being vulnerable is okay, in fact it takes courage – it is a strength to ask for help and accept our pain. She's putting **you've got the power** into practice and rocking it.

She is now ready to let herself be seen, even though there are no guarantees everything will go exactly how she wants. She is accepting herself and her life and feeling grateful for all the wonderful family, friends and things she has in it. That's elixir worth having.

Well done, Olivia, enjoy your celebration - you deserve it, you've done an amazing job. We love you and know your transformation and success from this journey will light the way on your future missions. **You've Got the Power.**

CONCLUSION

Clearly, **you've got the power**, too!

By now, you should have a good idea about how following your heart can create the life of your dreams. You've learnt many things and faced many fears, and we love you. You are able to connect the idea that your inner spirit is true power in the world. By embarking on your hero's quest, you've experienced the feeling of being alive, of taking risks and owning your power.

You've Got the Power has provided you with the tools you need to see past the worries and fears which hold you back. I trust that you've learnt in the end that you are the source of all your own power and happiness. You see, in life we all must overcome many obstacles and challenges – no one else can do it for us; in the end we are our own life coach. Of course, it's great to connect and get help along the way, we don't deny this, but I repeat it is you who makes the magic become manifest in your life through daring to create your dreams.

I celebrate the start of your new life. Use your elixir of love, wisdom, knowledge and freedom to continue to support yourself, your friends and your family and create great change in the world.

When we watch *Star Wars* or *The Wizard of Oz* or any great heroic story, we love it because we can see a bit of ourselves in the hero. We love following the trials of the hero, on his or her journey, in these epic adventures, because they make us feel alive. In fact, Joseph Campbell himself (who influenced George Lucas) said, '**I don't believe people are looking for the meaning of life as much as they are looking for the experience of being alive.**'

Ultimately, you, our amazing hero, have returned to where you started, but things will clearly never be the same again. Now that you know yourself, what you want and how you can share in the world, it is now your responsibility to use this knowledge to rock the world. Remember, as your life changes, your vision may change with it. Don't be afraid to think big. Your mission may be to change the world, but first you may have to change yourself.

Keep growing and shining your power – with love – until the next time ...

Paula

LIST OF CHARITIES AND SUPPORT GROUPS

BARNARDO'S

0208 550 8822

A children's charity that protects and supports the UK's most vulnerable children and young people.

THE CHILDREN'S SOCIETY

0300 303 7000

A charity offering life-changing support for vulnerable children and young people.

CRUSE BEREAVEMENT CARE

0808 808 1677

A charity offering a free national helpline offering emotional support to anyone affected by bereavement. It also has a website for young people – Hope Again – where you can learn from other young people and how to cope with grief, and feel less alone: www.hopeagain.org.uk.

NSPCC CHILDLINE

0800 1111

A free national helpline for children and young people in trouble or danger. Its aims are to fight for childhoods, protect those at risk and prevent child abuse.

RETHINK YOUR MIND

0808 808 4994

A not-for-profit project whose purpose is to creatively express well-being through its national and personalised resources – The Yellow Book is available in schools, containing well-being and recovery material from various sources and signposting to national organisations and charities of support.

YOUNG MINDS

020 7336 8445

A charity that provides information and advice for anyone with concerns about the mental health of a child or young person.

Would you like to teach these well-being concepts to the Young Minds around you?

Train to Teach with us
Join our SMART Young Minds Team

Join the revolution for a brighter future for our kids and let your passion and purpose shine.

SMARTfoundations
Institute of Mindful Well-being Teacher Training

Contact us:

 www.smartfoundations.co.uk